For Phoenix!

love
xo
Cindylou ,

2014

CAVE WALL GRAFFITI
FROM A
NEANDERTHAL COWBOY

BY BAXTER BLACK
ILLUSTRATIONS BY WALLY BADGETT

Copyright ©2014 by Baxter Black

Published by: Coyote Cowboy Company
PO Box 2190
Benson, AZ 85602
baxterblack.com

Cover and book design by Becky Harvey

LIBRARY OF CONGRESS CATALOGING IN PUBLICATION DATA:

Main entry under:
Cowboy Poetry

Bibliography: p
1. Cave Wall Graffiti from a Neanderthal Cowboy
2. Poetry-Cowboy
3. Cowboy-Poetry
4. Humor-Cowboy

I. Black, Baxter, 1945-
Library of Congress # 2014943055
ISBN-13: 978-0939343-59-1

OTHER BOOKS BY BAXTER

The Cowboy and His Dog
A Rider, A Roper, And A Heck'uva Windmill Man
On The Edge Of Common Sense, The Best So Far
Doc, While Yer Here
Buckaroo History
Coyote Cowboy Poetry
Croutons On A Cow Pie
The Buckskin Mare
Cowboy Standard Time
Croutons On A Cow Pie, Vol 2
Hey, Cowboy, Wanna Get Lucky? (Crown Publishing, Inc.)
Dunny And The Duck
Cow Attack
Cactus Tracks And Cowboy Philosophy (Crown Publishing, Inc.)
A Cowful Of Cowboy Poetry
Horseshoes, Cowsocks And Duckfeet (Crown Publishing, Inc.)
Ag Man The Comic Book
Hey, Cowgirl, Need A Ride? (Crown Publishing, Inc.)
Blazin' Bloats & Cows On Fire!
The World According To Baxter Black: Quips, Quirks & Quotes
The Back Page (Western Horseman Books)
Lessons From A Desperado Poet (TwoDot)
Herbert's Night Off
Reindeer Flu
Ride, Cowboy, Ride! Eight Seconds Ain't That Long (TwoDot)
Poems Worth Saving

TABLE OF CONTENTS

INTRODUCTION

INTRODUCTION

The title of this book represents those of us cowboys who intend to become somebody's ancestor someday.

Our writings and pictures on cave walls will be studied, scrutinized and mused over by Third Millinium folklorists. They will ponder the purpose of horns on mammals. What did they use the long nylon cords for? Did the primitive animal caregivers, now known as Anamites, use any of the Protein Providers, 'Pro Pops' (formerly called animals) for anything but food?

They will look at 2015 cowboys as primitive. So much of what we understand and believe to be true today will barely be a footnote in a thousand years. The good part is, we get to be us today. A place in time that allows us to think our own thoughts without everybody being able to read your mind. A sky that is clear enough to see the stars. A relationship with nature's critters, large or small, that are not genetically modified clones. The opportunity to take a chance, and the God-given freedom to believe.

As for the future of cowboys, I suspect there will still be a place for them on the fringes of civilization. Places like Van Horn, Texas; Buffalo, Alberta; Douglas, Arizona; Cody, Nebraska. Anywhere you go where it would not be uncommon to hear, "Whattya mean I can't ride this horse? Ear'im down and stand back!"

This book is dedicated to Wendy P. Glenn, Rancher and Archaeologist (1940-2014), who showed me the writing on the wall.

The Beginning

ON CAVE PAINTING

Messages from our ancestors are pictured on cave walls. These precious drawings give us a sense of who they were. But it has always bothered me why most Neanderthal graffiti is so primitive, so juvenile?

Were there no artists among them who could make their characters look realistic?

Did not a single one know the way legs bent, or the shape of a buffalo, a foot or an antler? Surely through the centuries a frustrated art critic would have commented on the warrior's hands that looked like a Charlie Brown Christmas tree, or elk, deer or moose stick figures that looked like saw horses with mangled TV antennae on their heads. What is meant to be bears could easily have been armadillos, abandoned tires, an old disc blade, a carpet remnant or elephant spoor on a Tanganyika airstrip!

Was it because they were forced to use the tar-and-broken-limb medium? Were they limited by the size of the canvas? Was the lighting always bad?

AFTERTHOUGHT: *I guess now we know what excites Art History majors.*

6

ON WABI SABI

I was at the sale barn recently and heard one farmer say, "Feng Shui is passé."

"I know," said the other, stuffing a cabbage-sized wad of Red Man in his cheek, "Wabi Sabi is back."

By my definition Feng Shui represents neatness, clean lines, proper placement and harmony. Wabi Sabi embodies the idea that there is beauty in imperfection; that flaws enhance rather than detract.

So, you must be thinking, that means if my yard is covered in junk, then I must be practicing Wabi Sabi? Sorry, one of the rules: If you think the 'life experience' of the '96 Plymouth Neon makes your place more beautiful, that would be Wabi Sabi. But if you couldn't afford any better, or were just too lazy to move it off the blocks, then it would not.

Wabi Sabi is in the eye of the beholder.

AFTERTHOUGHT: *Wabi Sabi is actually prohibited in the Army, and among those artists who paint the yellow line on highways.*

ON MY GUITAR NAMED MARTIN

I would often take my guitar to the ranches where we were workin' cows. Sometimes the cowboys would join in. At one big outfit a prospector from Dublin often showed up with a mandolin, and he fit right in ... Martin spoke Irish! Who knew?! I took him to sheep camps, too. The herders couldn't speak English but they could understand Martin. We made a lot of miles together but he stayed with me. I took him places most folks wouldn't go with a gun!

He was with me through all those sad love songs, honky tonk songs, funny ones, bluegrass, country, cowboy, even the occasional gospel song. Every song I ever wrote, Martin heard it first.

AFTERTHOUGHT: *"This will be in the key of A for all our Canadian friends, or C for our Spanish speaking amigos, or G for those who are amazed." - Pinto Bennett*

ON BARNYARD BESTSELLERS

Herefords Are From Venus
Angus Are From Mars
An example of prehistoric rivalry.

Chicken Soup For The Newly Weaned
Ruminent's Soul
Heart wrenching stories of leaving home.

The 9 Steps To Parasitic Freedom
Say goodbye to lice.

Don't Sweat The Small Stuff
Shetlands improve their self esteem.

The Joy Of Artificial Insemination
Do the best with what you've got.

And lest you think ungulates don't read for fun, I offer
these last titles:

The Sheep Whisperer
The Cow From Snowy River
A Power Line Runs Through It
Feedlots Of Madison County
The Dairy Of Ann Frank

ON WHY COWBOY POETRY IS FUNNY

It's the reason us cowboy poets
write our humorous refrains.
'Cause like I said it's either laugh or cry.

For example, let's say yer horseback
in the sortin' pen one day
And see a friend go flyin' through the sky!

We'd all quick go ridin' over where
he'd bucked off in the dirt
To check his pulse, if there's still one to raise.

And...if he's livin' you start tellin' the story right away,
And if he's dead you wait a couple days.

AFTERTHOUGHT:

I was desperate for a rhyme in "Boat Roping,"

*"He grabbed an oar, shoved away and started paddling
wildly . . . then rowed himself out to the cow, who watched
him . . . ? Well . . . how 'bout crocodiledly?"*

ON TOUGH vs. STRONG

There is a difference between being *TOUGH* and being *STRONG*. A 600 lb roping steer is tough, a 2000 lb Brahma bull is strong. A strong man can lift 100 lb bags for an hour. A tough man can lift 50 lb bags all day.

There is a difference between being *FAST* and being *QUICK*. A 747 is fast, a fruit bat is quick. Fast people are handy to send after things, to deliver the mail, and to walk dogs. Quick people are good at catching house flies, stealing 2nd base, and dealing cards.

There is a difference between being *INTELLIGENT* and being *SMART*. An intelligent person knows how many brussel sprouts it takes to fulfill the average daily requirement of vitamin K. A smart person knows nobody eats them!

I like to think of myself as a Corriente steer who likes brussel sprouts but who gets caught stealing 2nd base!

AFTERTHOUGHT: *I was chastised by my family for damaging Grandma's Bowflex. An example of being stupid or being dumb?*

ON CLONES FROM HISTORY

The Sheriff of Nottingham, robbed from the rich and poor alike and had no conscience. He could be recloned as an IRS agent.

Lewis and Clark, managed to make it across the country by trading trinkets to keep from getting shot. Animal Health salesmen.

Buffalo Bill, a showman, took advantage of the cowboys and stayed one jump ahead of the creditors. He could easily slip into the boots of a rodeo producer.

A Roman Slave: He could own his own dairy!

Finally, Moses, lost for 40 years wandering in the wilderness with no apparent means of support: simple, a professional team roper.

AFTERTHOUGHT: *I said, "Enjoy yourself." He said, "I'd rather do that than not enjoy myself. I do that all the time."*

Cowboy Up

ON TYIN' A GREEN BROKE HORSE TO THE OLD GRAY MARE

Ray called Johnny Boy to help him start a pigheaded gray filly. Ray's plan was to tie her to Johnny's big brown horse; 15 1/2 hands, #2 shoes, sired by Kenworth.

Gray was saddled and haltered. Johnny mounted Brownie and tied Gray's halter rope to his saddle horn with a 2 foot lead. Ray climbed on Gray, Johnny Boy dropped Brownie into Compound and let out the clutch. The filly set her feet and skidded like a 4-leg-ged skier on the bunny tow.

Then she exploded! She sprang at the sideways Brownie, left front foot across the swells, right front across the cantle! Ray dove one way, Johnny the other! She stripped the saddle off over Brownie's head and drug it around the pen, managing to stomp and slash her signature into the new leather.

Johnny Boy stood there dumbfounded. Ray had noogies, his brand new Bona Allen saddle looked like something a Tyranosaurus threw up and his shirt was torn down the back in two pieces, each with a sleeve.

Ray couldn't hear all of Johnny Boy's compliments about his filly, because his ears were filled with sand. Probably just as well.

AFTERTHOUGHT: *Giving your horse to a good trainer is like letting a butcher sharpen your pocket knife.*

ON THE DEFINITION OF A COWBOY

"Someone who can replace a uterine prolapse in a range cow in the middle of a three section pasture with nothing but a horse and a rope."

The first thing that defines a cowboy is that he is there, on the scene, on duty to herd, guard, protect, serve and save the cow. To do this he must be able to restrain the beast. He must be able to approach the cow horseback, capture her and hold her so the ailment can be examined.

I remind people that even though range cows are domestic animals, they are not tame. They're like K-Mart employees, you can't actually walk up to one.

Then the cowboy is required to treat the ailment, be it a prolapse, wire around the foot, a sick calf in the Palo Duro Canyon, the Tonto Basin or the Alvord Desert, it's still cowboy, horse and rope. The basic essentials.

I've overheard people compare the abilities of trick ropers, bronc riders, horse trainers and veterinarians to those of the *workin' for wages* cowboy. That he is not as accomplished in his individual skills as they are. They seem disappointed.

I remind these folks that they are not professional cowboys . . . they just do it for a living.

AFTERTHOUGHT: *You never know if you need a cowboy, until a cowboy is all you need.*

15

ON THE ANATOMY OF A WRECK

Very few bronc riders could have stayed on and Paddy was not one of them. There was a scream like someone falling off a cliff, followed by what might have been a giant zipper being opened, two thuds, a whomp and a crumple!

The horse regained his feet, unhurt. Ten feet away Paddy appeared to be standing on his head, shirt down around his shoulders, boots sticking up in the air and completely pantless! He keeled over like a felled tree.

During the cleanup they deduced that when Paddy was ejected he must have hung his belt buckle on the saddlehorn, because his jeans were torn completely off his body. It took two of them to pull his hat back off his nose and a set of wire cutters to get the sagebrush out of his ear.

The lady who told me the story was an artist but she'd never been able to paint the picture. She said she couldn't ever get the flames right.

AFTERTHOUGHT: *"He attempted an emergency dismount!"*
- Ross Knox

ON THE IOWA COWBOY

"Where were you born?" the reporter asked one of my Colorado cowboy friends.

"Iowa." he answered

"Iowa!" she said, "Why did you move?"

"Because it's hard to be a cowboy in Iowa."

AFTERTHOUGHT: *Roping Vs. Tilt Table -*

Roping and dragging calves to the branding fire . . . compared to running them down a narrow alley with a broken plastic whip, catching them in a clanking calf chute and then flipping them on their side . . . is the difference between shooting a pheasant out of the air or hitting one with your car.

That's what horses were invented for.

ON BUTCH AND CHOPE

Chope roped a snortin' bad bull and tied on. The bull hit the end of the line and lifted his front quarters off the ground like Trigger. The saddle horn broke off and flew like Mickey Mantle drivin' one over the center-field fence!

It cracked like a gun shot, just missed a dismounted cowboy and hit another horse who bucked loose and broke his reins! The bull galloped off draggin' the line.

Butch looked back to see Chope madly tyin' another rope to his saddle through the gullet.

"Whatya doin'?" asked Butch.

"I'm gonna rope him and get my rope back," said Chope.

Butch stared at him. His broken saddle seat sat cock-eyed, his hat was gone. You could almost hear his ears ringin'. It was like Chope was lashing himself to the end of a harpoon line.

Butch placed his hand over Chope's and said, "Let's think about this a minute . . . nobody's dead yet."

AFTERTHOUGHT: *Cowboys come in parts.*

ON ROUGH COUNTRY

We'd started into some rough country, brand new to the cattle. I felt like Lewis and Clark! Two miles later, over big tracts of creosote bush and whitethorn I could see a large cut bank where the water tank was. I had a vision of Moses looking over the Grand Canyon and thinking . . . "We're almost there!"

By the time we got back to the horse trailer my nose was running, my knee was swollen, my shirt looked like I'd been in a sword fight. There was a gouge on my right arm, a slash across my cheek and a memory of my wore-out horse trying to roll in the muddy tank with me still in the saddle. I guess he just didn't appreciate the glory of cowboyin'!

AFTERTHOUGHT: *"Oh give me land, lotsa land under starry skies above . . . Don't fence me in!"*

19

ON WHY A COWBOY NEEDS A COW

A cowboy needs a cow,
like a sailor needs a plank,
Like a blister needs a toe hold,
Like a robber needs a bank.

A cowboy needs a cow brute
Like a pack mule needs a crup.
Like a stuntman needs an actor,
Like a catcher needs a cup.

I say a cowboy needs a cow,
They're joined at the hip.
Politicians and reporters
Have the same relationship.

Without each other to torment,
They don't know where to start
Like criminals and lawyers
You can't tell them apart!

So to those who think I'm whining
That I'm pitiful and sad
That I'm just another loser
Throwing good love after bad,

It's not all that one-sided,
As I've learned in therapy
'Cause my cow finally admitted
That she really needed me.

AFTERTHOUGHT: *I tried to teach my favorite cow to write free verse. I gave up. She never learned to punctuate.*

20

COWBOY MENTALITY

ON WOMEN WHO LOVE COWBOYS

I have concluded that women who marry a "cowboy-type" suffer from a genetic defect. One that blocks out good judgement.

My concern is if this chromosomal defect was corrected, would she be able to see our 'misguided priorities'? Like missing the birth of our first child because we had to go roping? Or our 'belligerent stubbornness' of insisting that there is still gas in the gas tank even though the gauge says *empty!* Or our 'uncouthness' when we insist on explaining the difficulties of replacing a uterine prolapse to our new in-laws, who are both Presbyterian ministers?

But on the good side, as long as this defect remains intact in a certain number of females, cowboy types will always have a chance. We will always be able to begat little cowboys. And who doesn't love little cowboys!

AFTERTHOUGHT: *The plan was simple, like my brother-in-law Phil. But unlike Phil, this plan might work.*

ON THE CLOTHES HORSE

I'm the kinda cowboy who gives Wrangler a bad name. It's not that I don't try on each pair before I buy. You have to! Maybe I'm just odd shaped, hard to fit. They do make one style of Wranglers that have legs that fit tight around a shovel handle, which I appreciate. My calves are so scrawny I have to tamp dirt in my boots to hold them on!

But no matter how skinny they make the pantlegs, the seat still bags. When I finally do get'em on, I give the appearance of a swing set somebody tried to gift wrap!

AFTERTHOUGHT: *I was visiting with an ol' timer after he had seen me doing my cowboy poetry show. "What did you think?" I asked.*

He said, "With that shirt and moustache and your hat pulled down over your ears, you look like a cross between Porter Wagoner and Dennis Rodman."

ON LEAVING A DEEP IMPRESSION ON A DATE

Don was trying to impress his date one dark night, by demonstrating the proper technique to pull a calf. She sat in the pickup as he approached the cow in the headlights. The cow rose and attacked him! After he executed a complete cartwheel and landed on his back the possessive mama cow mowed him down!

Don climbed back in the cab and tried to regain his composure and recapture the mood by explaining that he had been "in control" the whole time.

However it was not very convincing what with the big glob of manure plastered on the side of his neck and the piece of placenta dangling from his ear.

AFTERTHOUGHT: *It's hard bein' a cowboy. If a man gets run over by a truck he gets sympathy. If he gets run over by a cow, everyone laughs.*

ON COWBOY LOVE

You can call me a romantic, even pansy if you choose.
It's not the cowboy image that the movie moguls use
But, beauty's in the eye of the beholder, so we're told
A flower to a botanist, a fungi to a mold

Tight jowls and big firm hineys
Is a pork producer's dream
Clear water to a plumber,
To a vampire it's a fleam

But, to a cowboy makin' long days
Checkin' fence and water gaps,
His idea of perfection,
His triple decker, shoot the moon,
Till death doth he collapse
His Venus on the half shell, is a woman wearing chaps!

AFTERTHOUGHT: *"She's wormed, fresh offa wheat grass and showin' a little ear."*

Misinterpretation: A modest stripper on an organic diet has swallowed her chewin' tobacco.

ON PARDON ME!

I was at a rodeo recently and saw a woman take matters into her own hands. She was sitting behind a cowboy wearing a big hat. She tapped him on the shoulder and said, "Young man, I cannot see around your hat. Would you mind removing it." He explained that it was improper for a cowboy to remove his hat at a rodeo except for the National Anthem.

But she had made her point, so I just traded places with her.

AFTERTHOUGHT: *"Every time I turn my head like this, it hurts my neck!"*

"Well, duh . . ."

ON COWBOY VOCABULARY MISCONCEPTIONS

"My whole flock has keds." MISINTERPRETATION: Sheep are now endorsing tennis shoes.

"I work in a hog confinement facility." MISINTERPRETATION: She teaches classes in the campus jail at U. of Arkansas.

"I prefer the Tarentiaise over the Piedmontese." MISINTERPRETATION: He is picky about cheese.

"Do you know where I can get a bosal, romal and some tapaderas?" MISINTERPRETATION: I'd suggest someplace that sells Mexican food.

"I heard that Speed Williams and Rich Skelton got one down in 5-flat." MISINTERPRETATION: Must be a couple of quick anesthesiologists!

"I heard that Texas is now Brucellosis free." MISINTERPRETATION: I assume Bruce, who is of Greek origin, finally got a good lawyer.

"You can stick a fork in me." CORRECT INTERPRETATION: "I'm Done!".

ON HINTS FOR THOSE SEEKING THE JOB OF HIRED MAN

Expensive equipment doesn't guarantee you'll be paid well. That's where the money all goes!

If the words "day off" or "insurance" bring a quizzical look to the boss's face, better think it through.

If the prospective employer complains he can't keep a hired man on the place, BEWARE!

If the boss lives in a 1992 New Moon single-wide, don't expect much from his offer of "housing furnished." BACK OFF.

The most successful arrangement I've seen was Tom and Dale. Tom said, "Wouldn't nobody else work for Dale and nobody else would hire me. I've got a job for life!"

ON LOOKING FOR A POSITION

I worked for a man whose education came from experience. He harbored a suspicion of new college graduates seeking employment who overestimated their own value. He invariably, would bring in resumes, deposit them on my desk and say, "This is another one of those guys who wants a position. Tell him all we've got is jobs!"

ON THE COST OF RECYCLING

We try to be recyclers. Yesterday I noticed our toilet paper was labeled "100% unbleached, 100% recycled paper, 100% post-consumer content and 59.4 sq ft in total area."

It's a little like newsprint and I feel odd using toilet paper somebody else has used, but I guess we're doin' the right thing.

At least I have the satisfaction of using environmentally correct antique toilet paper. I can envision the historical significance of knowing it may have been used by Davy Crockett, Horace Greeley or Chief Sitting Bull. And if that don't make it worth the price, I'll send you a couple of used corn cobs!

AFTERTHOUGHT: *When you tell your buddy, "Scuze me a minute, I'm gonna slip around behind this tree and relieve myself." How do you know it's the back of the tree?*

ON IF THIS OL' HAT COULD TALK, IT'D TELL A MILLION STORIES

IF THIS OL' HAT COULD TALK, "I did my share of fanning a bronc, dippin' water from the creek, and shading a good ol' cowboy's eyes."

How 'bout IF THIS OL' SOCK COULD TALK? "I've laid for days between his gnarled foot and the sole of his stinkin' boot. It's like being stuck to the bottom of a dumpster."

IF THIS OL' MOUSTACHE COULD TALK, "I feel like a rest home for migrating lice, a birdhouse for nesting gnats, a picnic table for the common housefly. I get gnawed on, tugged and twirled so much I feel like an easy date."

IF THIS OL' POCKET COMB COULD TALK, "If I lose one more tooth I'm gonna have to get an upper plate."

IF THIS OL' SHIRT POCKET COULD TALK, "Next time he puts a half-chewed cud of Redman in me while he's havin' lunch, I'm gonna prolapse in his bowl of Chili!

IF THIS OL' PLASTIC SLEEVE COULD TALK . . .

AFTERTHOUGHT: *A friend will always tell you if your hat's on backward.*

ON MOUSTACHE REGULATIONS

1. The owner and operator of said moustache shall confine him (or her) self to long foods, i.e. hot dogs, spaghetti, eels or breadsticks. Wide foods such as watermelon, corn on the cob or BBQ beef ribs are prohibited.

2. Width of ornate handlebars shall not be wider than state-regulated handicap door width.

3. Use of hallucinogenic drugs, garlic, or catfish bait as adhesive or stiffening agents are disallowed.

4. Renting of space to lint collectors, real estate agents or mascara testing shall be prohibited.

5. Excessive self-fondling of facial hair is discouraged to reduce vanity, preening disease and dandruff dissemination.

And remember, always wear your moustache responsibly, treat it as a loaded weapon, because even on the lip of an experienced practitioner, it can go off accidentally.

AFTERTHOUGHT: *Caution - To eat corn on the cob you must roll it backwards or it gets up your nose.*

ON WELL, DUH

I remember years ago, one snowy winter morning I took a shortcut across the sagebrush flats from Grandview, Idaho to Boise. I got stuck.

I called Harold, the truck dispatcher and told him I needed a pull. He said, "That road's closed!" I said, "I know, I had to move the 'ROAD CLOSED' sign to get on it."

Well, duh . . .

AFTERTHOUGHT: *"Life is tough, and it's really tough if yer stupid." - Damon Runyon*

ON OVERCOMING FEARS

I stood on the edge of a grain elevator and watched some ravens fly below me. Just watching made my stomach sink. I thought, 'Wouldn't it be awful to be a bird and be scared of heights?'

It's as bad as being a claustrophobic mole!

I've know cowboys who were afraid of horses, horses that were afraid of veterinarians, veterinarians who were afraid of cowgirls, cowgirls who were afraid of cows, cows that were afraid of cow dogs, and cow dogs that were afraid of thunder.

Most of us deal with our fears.

Steve and I were watching ships at sea one afternoon off the California coast. I remarked that I had read that many sailors in the old days couldn't swim. Steve mulled it over a moment, then said, "The good side is, it probably made them better sailors!"

AFTERTHOUGHT: *Just because it isn't true doesn't mean you can't believe it.*

ON THE REUNION OF THOSE WHO DARED

Who said you can't live life over
Who said you can't bring back the past.
Who said you can't relight the eternal flame
Of memory and make it last.

Gosh, it was great while it lasted
Nobody could ride'm like us
Like rockets on fire we shot for the moon
It was win or die tryin' or bust.

We brought ourselves back from the ashes
Set Phoenix's tail on fire,
We reran the race for old times sake
And finished it under the wire.

So, don't tell me it can't last forever
'Cause where there's a will there's a way
But, in fact forever don't matter
Much as makin' it last one more day.

AFTERTHOUGHT: *"I have reached that age where the things that I remember most clearly, never even happened."* - *Mark Twain*

Rodeo

ON TWO JUMPS

Now, all the young bronc stompers
and bullriders knew Lecille.
A rodeo clown and hero to all who strapped on the steel.

Lecille knew the bulls and broncs
and always offered advice
On rodeo, on love and life, on learnin' sacrifice.

Two Jumps was pullin' his bullrope,
the rosin startin' to smoke
When Lecille looked over the chute gate,
squinted his eyes, then he spoke.

"Two Jumps," Lecille confided,
"To really make yourself proud,
Ain't no way you can ride this bull . . .
so hang up and thrill the crowd!"

AFTERTHOUGHT:

Why do some people become rodeo clowns?

Same reason some dogs chase cars.

ON CHAMPION COWGIRL

Ted called the other day to report that his 8 year old daughter has announced she's going to become a barrel racer. Her first request was for a real horse trailer. The 16 foot stock trailer with the cow manure floor and faulty wiring would not suffice now that she'd made her career choice.

Ted related all this with the whipped-dog attitude who had just found out his new mother-in-law was a chronic sleepwalker and would be moving in with them.

"Didn't you go to the National Finals Rodeo?" I asked.

"Yeah," he said, "but she can't rope or ride broncs."

"Do you know who won the most money?"

"The All Around, I guess." he said.

"Nope, the barrel racer," I said.

"Humm... maybe she'd like a Featherlite..."

AFTERTHOUGHT: *I can see the movie now, "The Lipstick and the Spur!"*

ON TEAM ROPER'S CREDIT CARD

Carl told me the other day that one of his team roping buddies boasted he'd gotten a platinum credit card. I was taken aback! It was like being told that a serial killer had been granted knighthood, or the starling had been named the state bird of Idaho!

Turns out he didn't get a loan, or sold a good horse (or stole a good horse), or donated his body parts for research. I was sure he didn't have a job. I took a long shot, he could have won a roping? No, guess not. If he didn't rob a bank, how'd he get it?

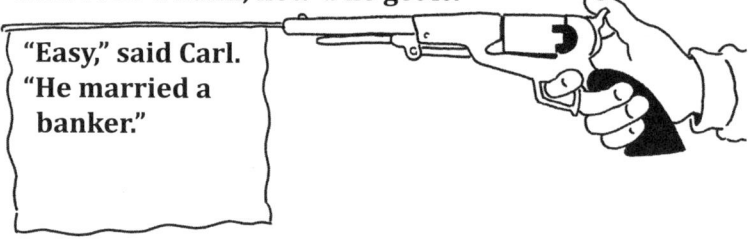

"Easy," said Carl. "He married a banker."

AFTERTHOUGHT: *Larry rode into the heeler's box. I asked him if he was riding a new saddle. "Yup," he said, "I used to ride broncs in it, Association tree. I just bolted this horn on and wrapped it with duct tape. George Strait gimme this halter!"*

ON RODEO CONTRACTORS

Rodeo contractors are an odd lot. They're not smilers. They're always on the job...sort of a cross between a prison guard and the captain on a pirate ship. Maybe it's because they are trying to maintain order in a sea of chaos. They are merely attempting to match up one cowboy with one animal, neither of which has been house broken. I've had the pleasure to be with several of them when they attempted to relax. Unfortunately, it's like watching Queen Elizabeth in her Bermuda shorts texting her broker at Billy Bobs!

ON COTTON ROSSER
RODEO CONTRACTOR

The ringmaster steps front and center.
The crowd begins to engage.
He brings us to a crescendo,
the rodeo arena's his stage.

So if you're askin' me what about him?
What he means to pro rodeo
I could say lots of things about Cotton,
But he dang sure puts on a show!

ON SADDLE BRONCS

Saddle Bronc Riding is considered the classic rodeo event. If the rider prepares physically and mentally, sets his gear to allow the maximum performance, coordinates his explosion from the chute, spurs in position and draws a good horse, I'm told it sometimes is as easy as it looks. A masterful ride is likened to making the calculations and firing a missile at an asteroid approaching the Earth's atmosphere at the speed of Pluto and redirecting its trajectory.

As opposed to Bareback Riding which is like shooting a monkey out of a cannon!

AFTERTHOUGHT: *I overheard two ol' bronc riders watching the bareback rider buck off over the horse's head, get punched in the dirt and run over by his horse. "That sure is a hard way to make a livin'," said one. "Yup," said the other, "and it's a hard way not to make a livin', too."*

ON A PERFECT SADDLE BRONC RIDE

Ridin' broncs is an eagle's wing. A prehistoric reckoning, a panther's pulse about to spring, a buckin' horse ballet.

Like skippin' rocks or tickin' clocks, an army tank with Mustang shocks, a magnum load with the hammer cocked, a moment caught in time.

Suspended there, this purist pair with Casey-Necktie savior faire, two poets in an easy chair, makin' ridin' rhyme.

And I'll make a stand that a good one can ride through a storm in ol' Cheyenne, a champagne glass in the hack rein hand and never spell a drop.

'Cause he's a strain of the ol' time

chain who'd ear'em down, grab a hank of mane, then swing above the hurricane and fan him till he stopped . . .

AFTERTHOUGHT: *If writing is buck shot, poetry is a bullet.*

ON BILLY'S BRONC RIDE

Out came Billy Etbauer, all 140 lbs of him, on a big bad bay named Smokeless Blood Brother. They catapulted into the arena. The next 8 seconds looked more like a bad billiards shot where the cue ball banks off the rail and knocks the ten ball through the front window. Or if you've ever seen anyone fall down a set of stairs, you'll get a picture of the team's trajectory.

Smokeless slammed Fearless Billy into the arena wall, then ricocheted across the arena, weavin' and buckin' while Billy was rockin' and swervin', feintin', and firin' till they crashed into the far end, ejecting Billy out over the dumbstruck calf ropers who were watching from safety behind the fence, realizing once again why they had chosen to participate in a timed event instead of a self-flagellating, pull-my-finger, teeth-rattling train wreck, where you wear a bullet proof vest, several bone screws and a felt hat!

AFTERTHOUGHT: *Billy needs a big sandbox to play in!*

ON JESS'S EARLY RODEO DAYS

One year Jess entered a Mule Rodeo in Boise City, OK. It was a spectacular show. The gate swung open before the mule rope was tight! He actually did ride the mule the required 8 seconds but managed to slap it multiple times with each and every free appendage including his chin and the soles of his feet, which disqualified him.

Jess made a complaint to the stock contractor, casting the blame on the inattentive gate opener. The contractor considered it, then refused his request for a reride. But he did offer him half the clown's pay if he'd do it again!

AFTERTHOUGHT: *He didn't know what he was doing, but he never doubted he could do it!*

ON HEY, COWGIRL, NEED A RIDE?

You can talk about the glamour
And the love of rodeo
The challenge and the heartbreak
Of the dally and the throw
Of the guts and luck and glory,
The leather and the sweat
The gristle and the power
Of the bull that ain't rode yet
The vision of the buckle
Worn by superhuman champs
And paid for in contusions
Broken bones and aches and cramps
The siren's call of rodeo
That beckons one last ride
The gambler's itch, the mountain top
The pinnacle, the pride
The reason they give all they have
Is measured in a score
A crowd, a millisecond,
Flag and timer, judge and roar
But for some the lure is simpler
The attraction that still pulls
Like me . . . just gettin' girls
Was the reason I rode bulls!

AFTERTHOUGHT: *I used to ride bulls till my brains came in.*

ON DYIN' AND COMIN' BACK TO LIFE

Have you heard of those folks who have died and come back to life?

They describe it as being in a long dark tunnel with a light at the other end. I was there! I bucked off a bull, made a two point landing, broke my shoulder and knocked me out.

I was layin' there in the arena and seein' stars. I thought I heard birds chirping but that might be a Disney movie I'm getting mixed up with.

I was in a long dark tunnel with a light at the other end. I squinted my eyeballs and concentrated on the light and I realized . . . I was peekin' out through a button hole so I pulled my shirt back down, crawled back on the fence and snuck off.

AFTERTHOUGHT:
All my clothes are laundry. - Pinto Bennett

ON SHAWN'S STORY

I met Shawn in Utah. He had both his wrists in a cast "How did it happen?" I asked. It went like this:

He was leaned out over the northwest quadrant when the buckin' horse came down front feet first. Our cowboy was fired into the ground like a javelin. The horse thundered on by.

Cowboys rushed to Shawn's aid as he lay there like a drug runner's Cessna nose-dived into a plowed field in south Florida. Shawn finally managed to stand and recover his Marlboro Man mystique.

"You hurt?" they asked.

"No, I'm fine." he said.

"Look at your arms!" the crowd gasped.

Shawn said they curved up mid-forearm like a camel's foot.

"Man," I said, "What a wreck. Everything that could go wrong did."

Shawn nodded his head and started to walk away, then turned and said, "Did I tell ya he stepped right square in the middle of my new hat?" He hadn't, but it did explain the asymmetrical Teton Mountain block, and the corrugated edge of the brim.

AFTERTHOUGHT: *I can't make up stories better than this!*

ON TEAM ROPING HANDICAPS

Team ropers are ranked in their skills from a #1 to a #12 like a golfing handicap.

Then there are ropers who are just plain handicapped, like a #1.5: Left-handers who rope left-handed and spend the rest of their life trying to get in position.

#-2: Consistantly poor ropers but so creative inventing excuses that they deserve some credit. "Did you see how close that was? I had'em both, I saw. The loop must have snagged on a gum wrapper and it broke my concentration just as my horse switched leads, and in this humidity...blah...blah...blah."

#4F: Usually mature ropers who suffer rotater cuff injuries, bursitis, tennis elbow, carpal tunnel syndrome or other maladies that result in unusual roping styles, such as *one swing, wince and toss* like they're trying to get a booger off their finger.

#12.5: A poorly dressed cowboy, ridin' a scruffy horse needing a mane roaching and tail pulling, carrying a rope that looks like it spent the winter holding down tarps, bummin' Copenhagen and wanting to sleep in your trailer . . . who can rope better than most of us can write our name.

ON PIZZA VS. TEAM ROPER

Q. What's the difference between a twelve inch pepperoni pizza with everything on it and a team roper?

A. The pizza can feed a family of four.

ON A CALF ROPER

Out of the clear blue of the Western Sky
Like a dive bomber, target in the crosshairs,
Comes the equivalent of the dog fighting ace.

Tuned in like a torpedo on a string . . .
Whap-slap-two wraps and a hooey,
Faster than the eye can see.

In timed events you often hear folks ask,
"Where did it go?"
Like right before their very eyes
somebody stole the show.

But ropin' calves is sleight of hand
and magic ain't a crime,
So all he's really guilty of
is stealin' precious time.

AFTERTHOUGHT: *"He's so good, he likes to practice!"*
- *Jim Schafer*

ON WHY DOES AMERICA NEED COWBOYS

1. So the Press will know how to describe people who don't mind taking the handoff and running over the middle on a 4th down and 2 to go.

2. To serve as one of the few sources of amusement in the life of a cow.

3. To remind you of what you can become if you don't do well in math, English or study hall.

4. To act as a buckle bunny magnet.

5. To serve as inspiration for all the Charlie Russell, Roy Rogers and Louie L' Amour wannabees.

6. To prove that no matter how good you are at something, you can always get bucked off!

7. To serve as an example of a job description that is routinely excluded from actuary lists as "most dangerous, lowest paid, longest hours, and life expectancy" . . . because they can't afford insurance anyway! I mean, who would insure a boot jack, a plastic whip or a rubber hubcap hammer?

And finally, America needs cowboys for the same reason we need knights, punt returners, banjo players and Marines. You have to have someone you can send in first.

ON THE TOOTH FERRY

An older couple sat at the cafe counter in Hooper, NE. He had a hamburger cut in half on his plate. His sweet wife sat next to him patiently, with nothing in front of her. A stranger walked in, observed, and in a moment of generous compassion, he offered to buy the missus her own burger.

"No, thank you," said the old man, smiling, "We share everything."

The stranger went and washed his hands. Upon returning his heart swelled and he offered again. "Thank you, but no." answered the old man. "As I said, we share everything."

The frustrated stranger turned to the sweet lady. "Wouldn't you like your OWN hamburger?"

"Thanks anyway, sonny. I'm waiting for the teeth!"

AFTERTHOUGHT: *"I have done so much for so long with so little, I can now do almost anything with nothing."*
- *Walt Woodard, still a team roper . . . a heeler.*

50

Equisistitation

ON HORSE PEOPLE

There is a certain kind of person that ranks in my mind with duck hunters. Don't get excited, I'm not gonna say anything about duck hunters. After all, what can you say about someone who gets up in the middle of the night, in the middle of the winter, then goes out and stands in water all day, up to his . . . buckle, then shoots a duck. But, I'm not talkin' about duck hunters, no, I'm talkin' about horse people.

You may have one in your family. You know it when you sit down at the table with a horse person because the first thing they start talkin' about is horses. On and on and on.

And cowboys are the worst. You'll be drivin' down the road and pass a big ol' meadow with 52 sorrell geldings, each with one stocking leg and a snip right on the end of his nose. And the guy in the middle will say, "See that one 17th from the left...I broke him in 2010." How do you argue with somebody like that?

Or you go out to a friend's place and they say, "Doc, it's good to see ya! I just got a new horse! I know you'll wanna look at him!" See, they think because you're a veterinarian, that you care. Which, of course I really do!

AFTERTHOUGHT: *If you wonder if someone is a horse person, you don't have to scratch too deep to find out.*

ON EQUINE EGO

I was helping a man pick out a good cowboy hat. I explained wearing a good hat was a matter of pride. He protested that he wasn't a very good cowboy. "I just own a couple of horses. A cap is good enough for me."

"I didn't mean *your* pride! I meant the horse's!"

For those novice horsemen who don't think they are qualified to "dress the part"; hat, boots, rope, think of the damage they are doing to their horse's self esteem.

It's like putting the bridle on over the halter. Do you think the horse doesn't notice? It's like wearing your underwear outside your pants!

So do your part, good horsemen. Remember, in riding, just as in cooking, presentation is half the meal.

AFTERTHOUGHT: *"I never had a horse run away from me. I can ride as fast as any horse can run." - Ray Hunt*

ON WHY THE HORSE?

It's like asking why the sun. Why the heart? Why the color purple? If there were a monarchy, the horse would be King.

Without the horse the cowboy becomes a herder, Coronado would still be in Hermosillo, Napolean would have been an infantryman, and taxation without representation becomes the Sports of Kings.

Artists and photographers try to capture their spirit. *A stop-action photo of a dead run:* 1200 pounds balanced on one toe, fetlock extended, nostrils flaring, neck reaching, ears back, mane flying, tail flowing, eyes locked on the target and a human attached to the withers like a space shuttle tied to a rocket! It is no wonder that a horse can take our breath away.

The horse, amongst all other domestic beasts demands respect. They possess an intelligence that derives from being both predator and prey, hard and soft, brave and skittish, loyal and wary. They may feign to show some affection, but they don't pant and lick. Horses, after all, are royalty.

For that reason, I would propose that we eliminate the term "giddy up." Can you imagine walking up behind Queen Elizabeth or Ghenghis Khan and saying, "Giddy Up."?

AFTERTHOUGHT: *Why the goat? . . . never mind.*

ON WOMEN AND HORSES

It is no secret that the majority of horse clinic patrons are women. Psychologists might be able to explain the attraction of women to horses and vise versa, in more professional words but . . .

Maybe motherly instinct is involved, like a mom still telling her 46 year old son to keep his elbows off the table. Maybe she just needs attention and it's cheaper than a psychiatrist. Maybe she likes horses but doesn't like to rope or play polo or steeplechase and horse clinics is her hobby. After all, the horse might be her best friend, and who better to spend the weekend with.

For you men, I appreciate that many of you are horse people and, like me, enjoy the clinics. And for you ladies who like to ride, but could give a rat's pantaloons for the touchy-feely aspects the clinicians promote, I acknowledge the multitude of exceptions to my observations.

But I can't tell you how many times I've eavesdropped on horses talking to each other at the ranch, in dude string corrals, at training clinics, riding clubs, gymkhanas and horse shows, and what I hear repeated o'er and o'er is, "Oh, I don't know. She just understands me better."

AFTERTHOUGHT: *For my first (and last) Baxter Black horse training clinic I chose my theme song "Ghost Riders In The Sky" and "Hang and Rattle" as my catch phrase.*

I should have called it "The Harry Potter Hoedown." I know it works better at a tractor pull.

ON HORSE SHOW CONVERSATIONS

What they say . . .(what they really mean.)

"A fine lookin' horse you've got there
(if yer into modern art)

I had a horse like that one time
(but he wasn't very smart)

He seems a little bit feisty
(to have one foot in the grave)

Yup, I've used Ace myself sometimes
(when there's something left to save)

Good luck. I reckon yer up soon
(I'd hate to be in that wreck)

You've already finished your classes?
(And haven't broken your neck)

Two firsts and an honorable mention?
(Whoa up! I'm way off the trail!)

A fine lookin' horse you got there."
(maybe that sucker's for sale . . .)

AFTERTHOUGHT:

*A brand new super cab dually with a
3 horse slant - $72,340.00*

Two AQHA trained cutting horses - $29,905.00

One team penning buckle - priceless

ON MULE DAYS

I was in Bishop, CA at a grand celebration called Mule Days. There's a lot you can say about mule people; a good work ethic, patience, strong and very defensive about their preference for mules versus other beasts of burden like horses, llama, alpaca, camels, water buffalo, oxen and sherpas. They will talk for hours about the advantages of mules over four wheelers, brothers-in-law, a degree in psychology, and, of course, horses.

I was trying to explain Bishop Mule Days to a friend. I said it was kinda like a cowboy poetry gathering only more intellectual.

AFTERTHOUGHT: *Mules are like cats, they are just living at yer place, and doing as little as they can to get by, to stay there.*

ON LESSONS FROM A MULE MAN

There are two sides to mule people, the brainy side and the stubborn side.

They are deep thinkers mostly because they always feel the need to explain why they ride mules. This creates a natural stubbornness because mules are smarter than horses and mule people are indignant that everyone doesn't know that!

I worked for a mule man named John. He taught me three of life's lessons:

How to find your way when you don't have a map.
How to win the game when you don't know the rules.
And,
When somebody tells you it can't be done, what they really mean is "they can't do it."

AFTERTHOUGHT: *A horse is as good as a mule, till you need a mule.*

ON FLYNT'S TRADE

"Our first big trade!" he bragged to me.
"The start of our first million!"
The horse backed out and my first thought was
he looked somehow reptilian.

His ears had froze off near his head,
his legs bowed like a lizard
His back was humped, when he stepped out
his gait severely scizzored.

His head looked like a chest of drawers,
his lower lip, a shovel
And from the spur tracks on his side
I knew he might be trouble.

"Got him for a song," he said, "A bargain sure as I live."
"So, Flynt," I said, "I'm curious,
just what did you have to give?"

He turned to me, "A check," he said.
His eyes went kinda funny.
"Well," I said, "I'll give you this,
you sure got him worth the money!"

AFTERTHOUGHT: *"A human uses only
12% of their brain capacity!"*

"So what!"

ON IMPROVING MY HORSEMANSHIP

As I glance through my horse magazine I read bold print saying, "comfort, safety and style," "the world's largest," "the only school of its kind," "tested and proven," or "best ever made!" I am reminded that humans have been riding horses for millenia and everything we take for granted today, was once a brainstorm of some Mongolian or jolly ol' English knight's horse trainer.

"I don't know, Cedric . . . When I heft my lance, it pulls me over and I fall off."

"Funny, Sir Lancelot, I was just reading in the Camelot Horseman about a new piece of gear invented by a team roper in western Wales called a steer up, I'll check into it."

I've bought into many plans, pieces of equipment, sure cures and training videos. My friend Jack has aged some so he needs help getting on and off his horse. Being not too tall, doesn't help.

I was in Kanab, Utah and bought an EZ Stirrup Extender. "Perfect for Jack." I thought. It unlatches, lowers the stirrup 4 inches from the fender . . . after mounting lifts it back up, where it snaps into place.

We put it on his saddle. I asked him later how it worked. He said, "Great! I stood flat-footed and could put my left foot in the stirrup. The only problem I had was, when I went to swing over . . . I forked too soon!"

AFTERTHOUGHT: *"I train my horses with a 2x4, but they won't let me touch their head?"*

Well, duh . . .

ON WISDOM OF THE AGES

Grandpas have a special wish
And have since days of yore
To teach his children's children
Things their parents might ignore.
He has this kid upon a horse
As soon as mom allows
And fills him full of stories
'bout the ol' days punchin' cows.
So when the horse the kid was ridin'
Tossed him to the ground
The Grandpa said, "Now get back on,
Don't let him keep you down."
The boy balked but Grandpa knew
The lesson to be learned,
"One of us must ride this horse,"
he said, his voice stern.
Then wisdom passed from old to young
"Yer right," the kid said, true.
"You want I let the stirrups out
just one hole . . . or two?"

AFTERTHOUGHT: *Wisdom from the mouths of babes . . . is not always welcome.*

ON A HORSE MATTERS

I like living someplace where a horse matters.

I like being a person to whom a horse matters

I like being there when a horse matters.

I consider myself very lucky that I get to be a part of the wonderful world of horse sweat, soft noses, close calls and twilight on the trail.

I like living a life where a horse matters.

AFTERTHOUGHT: *Proverb: Work to a horse is anything he does because you make him do it.*

Vets and Dogs

ON ACTORS AND POETS AS NEIGHBORS

I have a friend who is a well-known actor but when we first met he was shoeing horses. I always appreciated that. Sure, he can act, but can he do anything? You bet! When the chips are down he can shoe your horse.

I went to vet school so when I graduated and went lookin' for a job and the prospective employer asked me, "What can you do?"

I could say, "I can fix your cow!"

Now days I'm an entertainer and my rhyming skills don't necessarily make me a better neighbor. I don't get many calls saying, "Bax, I've got a broken pipe in the shop and the water is up to my knees! Could you come over quick and . . . and . . . do us a poem?"

AFTERTHOUGHT: *Sometimes when people relive my cowboy poetry, they are wearing their 5 buckle overshoes!*

ON ANIMAL SIMILES

Strong as a lion, graceful as a gazelle, sly as a fox, crazy as a loon, cute as a bug's ear. Gentle as a kitten, mad as a hatter, fat as a tick, slicker than silk pajamas on a garter snake.

How 'bout plant similes? They fought like apples and oranges! Quit squashing around! What's good for the kumquat is good for the kudzu!

Snappy comebacks that "damn with faint praise,"
SMART AS: a trainload of sheep
              a wheelbarrow full of turkeys
              a busload of animal crackers
              a bucket of night crawlers

Or . . . witty as a team of oxen, charming as a fruit bat, clever as a cedar stump, cuddly as a centipede, ethical as a congress of millers, regular as a 3-toed sloth, loyal as a baseball team owner, welcome as head lice, romantic as a hippo's kiss, or handy as wings on a liver fluke!

All of which seem nicer than just saying, "Sometimes Baxter's dumber than boiled gravel!"

AFTERTHOUGHT: *I am living proof that you can write poetry with half your brain tied behind your back!*

ON A BAD SIGN

Pullin' a calf in the cattails!

I feel like a scuba diver, the calf hangs up at the hip.
I get his head on my shoulder.
It's hard to keep my grip,

He's slick as a new-born porpoise.
I heave him on the shore
And plop, right there in the water,
just glad there ain't no more.

The cow, relieved of her burden,
rises outta the crud
And walks the length of my body
mashin' me down in the mud.

My hat is the only thing floating,
I'm soaked from head to toe.
The cow is lickin' her baby
and watchin' me below.

I wait till he's up and suckin',
then slip out like a mouse
And thank the Lord
that I'm only half a mile from the house.

AFTERTHOUGHT: *When I put on a plastic sleeve and ran my arm inside a cow . . . I discovered a whole new world!*

ON COW EXTRACTOR

How many times has one of your cows got her foot stuck in a blender? Well, you need COW EXTRACTOR! It can xtract your cow out of: a womb, a deer blind, a Chevy Suburban, a snow bank, a pool hall, a portable dipping vat, a yard sale, a ten cow pile up, the neighbor's pasture, the neighbor's meat freezer, a flat bed, the Homecoming float, a sorting alley, loading chute, poetry gathering or a bad relationship.

No farm or ranch should be without a COW EXTRACTOR! As Joe from Okeechobee says, "I'VE TRIED IT ALL FROM WRECKING BALL TO DYNAMITE AND TRACTOR, BUT WHEN SHE'S STUCK I'VE HAD GOOD LUCK BY USING COW EXTRACTOR!"

AFTERTHOUGHT: *A veterinarian is like an offensive lineman, each knows that when he starts the day, that's as good as he's gonna look!*

ON VETERINARY ETHICS

Alas, some thought they saw a conflict going on
'tween his clinic and taxidermy shop
"These charges pain me deeply,"
he told his vet technician
"My reputation's always been the top,

What makes them think
I'd compromise my veterinary work
To make a little money on the side?"
"Well, they might be misinterpreting your heifer
calving price," she said,
"Not many charge a hundred and the hide."

AFTERTHOUGHT: *Dr. Terry DVM meant well. Of course, that was the same week he set a cat on fire. He remarked, "It's hard to blow out a Persian."*

Epilogue: The cat was only singed, thank goodness, and Dr. Terry is now a regulatory veterinarian.

ON CONCERNS FOR MODERN VETERINARY MEDICINE

1. The plethora of chickens - the dearth of chicken practitioners

2. Is there a place for grooming in an exclusive reptile practice?

3. Recipes for traditionally inedible species.

4. Are men in Vet Med a thing of the past?

5. What do you think of horses as house pets?

6. The future of leather shoes, purses, and seat covers made of dog hide.

7. The possibility of cat farming?

8. Do dogs have a Heaven?

9. Body piercing on domestic animals: fashion statement or cruelty?

10. Humane euthanasia techniques in an insect practice: squash or spray?

11. Alternative uses for cat hair, llama milk, ostrich feet, hoof clippings, Rocky Mountain oysters, and former large animal veterinarians.

AFTERTHOUGHT: *I watched two Mexican veterinarians spay 495 heifers in 5 1/2 hours . . . one every 45 seconds. Cost $10 a head. It made me ponder over the elaborate production we as veterinarians make over spaying a cat.*

ON DEATH BY WOODCHIPPER

During an eradication for Newcastle disease in chickens, a veterinarian used a woodchipper to kill and dispose of many thousands of affected birds.

He was criticized by the animal rights groups for cruelty. I talked to PETA's veterinarian.

To my mind the euthanasia method was virtually instantaneous and painless. No, she said, there was the apprehension of being killed and the pain when the blade of the woodchipper hooked her foot and drug her in.

EARTH TO PETA . . . EARTH TO PETA.

The blade is moving at 1200 revolutions per minute which is 20 revolutions per second.

How would she euthanize the birds? I asked.

Her approved method was to gas them in a special box. How many does it hold? I asked. 5, she said, comfortably. How long does it take? I asked. 15 minutes she said.

How do you dispose of the carcass? I asked. Bury them, or cremate them. And take them to the landfill? She didn't know, for sure.

I said, in this project they eradicated 30,000 chickens.

EARTH TO PETA . . . EARTH TO PETA.

AFTERTHOUGHT: *Even considering the IQ of poultry, the 26,000th chicken in line would have no clue what is coming. It's like, "cluck, cluck, cluck, say what?" BZZZZT!*

ON WHEN THE RUMEN GOES AWRY

I am a student of the cow. I have come to conclude that cows lead a fairly boring life. When I give them their sporadic weekly check, I think it's probably the high point of their day.

They graze, and when they are not grazing they are chewing their cud. The cud is part of a magnificent ruminant digestive process that allows cows to digest foodstuffs that are virtually indigestible to simple stomached animals, like people.

For instance, cows can derive nutritional benefit from eating lettuce! Who'd a'thunk it?! People eat lettuce, but people eat lettuce because it is the next best thing to eating nothing. Right! The best way to lose weight is to eat _____. No, not lettuce, the best way to lose weight is to eat nothing. But, nobody wants to eat nothing, so they eat lettuce . . . which is the next best thing.

AFTERTHOUGHT: *Wear a protective moustache cover when smoking among bloats, as methane will burn!*

71

ON BLOAT FROM A COW'S POINT OF VIEW

I had terrible stomach pains, a shortness of breath, then I slipped on the bank of the pond and went down. Next thing I remember were the two leg-ged, cowboy caregivers who come and disturb us now and then, manhandling me! One had a big rubber tube that he was forcing down my throat. It was dark. I felt dizzy, I couldn't see! I thought I was back in my sleeping bag!

I couldn't understand their two leg-ged cowboy talk but one was bawling and hollering and suddenly one of the caregivers' fingers caught on fire! There was a terrible explosion . . . I imagined I was a dragon or an F 16 or an industrial strength weed burner. The sky lit up!

And that is all I remember, that, and the caregiver baptizing himself in the creek.

AFTERTHOUGHT: *He doesn't have a lot to say but it takes a long time to find out!*

72

ON MACHO SURGERY

There's a practice in a practice of a vet who works on horses that embodies the machismo of their kind.

I was taught this ancient practice, cutting horses standing, meaning, both he and I were standing at the time.

To cognize the difficulty, the mule-headedness required to complete this task of surgery and cunning

One must grasp its greater meaning. It's often been compared to changing fan belts while the engine's running.

Or standing on a bar stool taking bets from one and all you can stick your head up through the ceiling fan

And never touch a single blade, or spill a drop of beer. The epitome of every cultured man.

AFTERTHOUGHT: *In cattle, the surgically removed body parts are called Prairie Oysters or Rocky Mountain Oysters. If extracted from equine I guess you could call them Pimlico Oysters, Buckin' Bronc Horse Balls . . . or Clydesdale Sliders!*

ON PET GUARDIANS

San Francisco has now joined Boulder, Berkeley and a few other helium-rich cities to outlaw ownership of pets. You may still have pets but they are no longer considered property, owners are now considered guardians.

The first word that comes to my mind is LAWYERS! I can see them lining up now; *"Your honor my client is suing his guardian, Mr. Pacelle, for cruel and unusual punishment. Once a year he is placed in a portable pet container and hauled to the veterinarian to have his anal glands expressed. It is humiliating, done without his permission and results in post expression blues.*

Expert testimony will be furnished by Daffy Duck and a renowned pet psychic who will translate for both. We are asking for a year's supply of Kibbles and Duck Chow for pain and suffering and $350,000 in expert and legal fees."

AFTERTHOUGHT: *In the land of the gelding the crypt orchid is king.*

ON HOMELESS DOGS

I drove by a professional homeless person again today. She's staked her corner at the intersection I take often and holds up a cardboard sign, "Need Help, God Bless."

She has a dog with her. I used to think the dog was a ploy for sympathy. But her life is not easy. 8 to 5, six days a week on that corner, then back to the hobo camp to sleep in a car.

Whatever she is, she isn't lazy.

Of late, I no longer think of the dog as a ploy. He's probably her best friend. Something, I suspect, she doesn't have in abundance. For her, like a lot of us, her dog lends some kindness and comfort in an often unsympathetic world. The dog, in return gets her love and protection.

Yup, she may be homeless, but her dog isn't.

AFTERTHOUGHT: *A mother let her young son name their new puppy. He named it "Arf."*

She said it was okay till he got older and started barking at the mailman. It was embarrassing to call him off! "Arf, Arf, Arf! Bad dog!"

ON JUST A DOG

Eulogy:

You were just a dog but you added to our life. Companion, listener, guardian and connection to a part of nature we tend to overlook because we're too busy worrying about the minutia of life. You reminded us to appreciate a sunny day, a bone to chew and a kind word. You'll be missed around here. You were just a dog. But you'll be in my heaven. Rest in peace, old friend.

AFTERTHOUGHT: *God bless all creatures, large and small.*

Cow
Bidness

ON A COWFUL

A cowful is a substantial quantity. 15 scoopfuls equal a cowful. Two bootfuls make a scoopful, two hatfuls would make a bootful. Half a hatful would equal a capful.

6 canfuls (as in beer can) makes a capful. One canful equals 40 thimblefuls, 20 teardrops in a thimbleful.

The dosage for penicillin would read: 4 teardrops per 5 scoopfuls of body wt. IM.

ON BACKWOODS MEASURE

A Missouri cowman was givin' me advice on pregnancy checking cows. "First thing," he said, "is sorting according to how big the calf is . . . " I'm thinkin' 30 days, 90 days . . . He said, "like squirrel, cat or beagle." I looked blank. "Big as a squirrel, big as a cat, big as a beagle, like that," he explained. He also claimed he could tell their sex if they were pretty far along. "How far along do they have to be," I asked. "Oh, say . . . big as a Mississippi channel cat!"

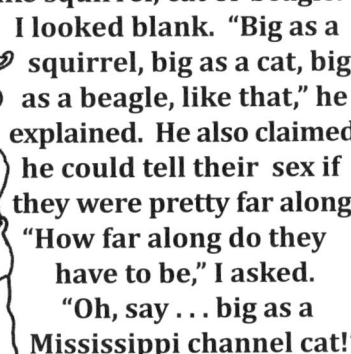

ON A BULL FIGHT

Then two bulls big as boulders
banged together head to head
It sounded like the closing of a vault.
Tectontic plates colliding, their reverberations spread
Like tremors from the San Andreas fault.

They pushed with heads like anvils,
bones as thick as two by fours
And circled, each one looking for a chance.
The ground beneath them pulverized,
like waltzing dinosaurs,
Triceratops reborn for one last dance.

AFTERTHOUGHT: *The bull jumped over the fence and bred the neighbor's cows. He was accused of practicing A.I.; accidental insemination!*

ON CULLING OLD COWS

If you don't have a place to go with your old gummer cows, here are a few alternative uses.

How 'bout County Fair Cow Rides, instead of Pony Rides they could be called Bony Rides.

Or, give them to Hindus with big yards.

Use them as guard animals near construction sites.

Take them as live bait on safaris or trolling for killer whales . . . no, not a good idea.

Rent them out to fertilize gardens, or towed behind a tanker jet for refueling practice.

Or, start your own retirement community; *"Send your venerable bovine to Broken Moo Cull Center! A complete care facility featuring a wading pool, calf visitation, Green Acres reruns, and activities such as cud ball, pin the tail on the coyote and synchronized estrus. Where they can spend their days recovering from defects until such time as they are suitable for that great McDonald's in the sky!"*

If it works we can move on to cull chicken retirement ranches. A place to spend their days just layin' and settin'. "Remember ladies, an egg a day keeps Campbell Soups away!"

AFTERTHOUGHT: *"He told me this old cow looked like she'd just come off the boat . . . I don't know if it was the Mayflower or Noah's Ark." - Jeff Rabon*

ON THE COW MAN AND HIS WIFE

Steve asked Penny to help him sort some big steers. "Where's Les?" she asked.

"Nobody's here," said Steve, agitated, "and I've got to sort them this afternoon."

Penny was put on the sorting gate. The alley was slick, the clouds were low, the wind blowing. It was 42 degrees.

"In," and "By," came the shouts from Steve as he orchestrated the train wreck. Cattle got passed, got cut the wrong way, the sorting gate got bent. Steve's instructions got louder and more pointed. Finally he chased one clear to the end of the alley cussing all the way!

He turned his frustrations on Penny and griped till he was blue. These cattle have to be worked, he couldn't do it alone. Why is it always like this, she's making a muck of everything, why can't she do it right?!

Penny stood, covered with green shrapnel, her rubber boots balled with mud and her hair stuck to the side of her head. She waited till Steve ran out of oxygen.

"So," she said, cutting him no slack, "Does this mean I'm fired?"

AFTERTHOUGHT:
Question - Why don't more cows run for president?
Answer - Because eight years seems like a lifetime!

ON CATTLE FEEDING ADDICTION

Cattle feeders are chronic gamblers. They thrive on the cold sweats, margin calls, sinking feelings and the exhilaration of guessing right. One year the market was so bad rumors were goin' around that some cattle feeders were considering shooting themselves. One desperate feeder called up several of his fellow cattle feeders in the area and left the message. "If you are contemplating suicide, would you do me a favor and shoot all your cattle first?" Thanx, Dallas.

ON WHO'S TO BLAME

The consulting veterinarian and the consulting nutritionist were discussing death loss with the feedlot manager. He came to the last one on the list; Hit By Truck.

"Obviously a trauma, therefore a medical problem," said the nutritionist. "Yes," said the vet, "but it was a feed truck, definitely nutritional in origin." "But as I recall," said the nutritionist, "they ran over him in the sick pen."

ON CATCHING A RIDE WITH A FAT CATTLE BUYER

My memory flashed back to the previous June when the market dropped and I was discounted $3 a hundred. I felt like I had helped pay for his car. It was a two seater high dollar Mazda Miata. But then it occurred to me, that it is only fitting, the Sheriff of Nottingham always rode good horses.

AFTERTHOUGHT: *Cattle buyers have come a long way from the old days when the nicest thing you could say was, "They are an example of why some mothers eat their young."*

ON THE FEEDLOT COWBOY

Life is just a bowl of cherries
to a first rate feedlot hand.
All the gates swing free and easy,
every day's precisely planned.

The boss is always pleasant
and lavish with his praise.
And when your wife demands it,
you get another raise.

All in all, they love their work.
The way their mufflers smell,
The Terramycin on their hands,
the Holstein steers from Hell.

Scoopin' out the rainy bunks,
a calvy heifer mess
And the profound satisfaction
when you lance a big abscess.

The glamour of their work
ensures an application glut
Though many hear the calling,
just a handful make the cut.

And he puts his heart into it and stays above the mob
So he don't have to give this up and get a real job!

AFTERTHOUGHT: *"Cowboys aren't strong on Holstein steers in the feedlot. It's hard to chase an animal that insists on following you!" - Kenny Eng*

ON THE BOOTS OF A SALESMAN

They've taken me a million miles; to farms, feedlots, dairies, ranches, irrigated fields, back doors, kitchen tables and pickups with the heater on.

These boots are made for WAITING; in the milk barn, the feedlot office, the shop, the vet's waiting room, leanin' on a pickup or on the mud porch. A good sales man has patient boots.

These boots love the road. Each trip is a fresh start, a new day. They let my mind escape from grumpy clients, snarly sales managers, late expense reports and last weekend at the trade show.

My boots are there listening to me formulate my sales pitch for my next call down the road. They hear me practice. If you can only be as good with the customer as you are in the front seat of your car!

So here I sit, waiting for my next appointment, flyers in hand, elbows on knees, boot toe tappin', tickin' like a two dollar watch, tuned and ready to be put on the line one more time, and I'm bettin' on me!

Yup, these boots fit me just fine.

AFTERTHOUGHT: *I expect to be paid what I'm worth but no one will hire me!*

ON THE COW DISTURBER

McGraw posed an interesting question. If a cowboy herds a herd of cattle, we call him a herder. If a sheepman herds a flock of sheep he's still a herder. Why isn't he a flocker?

Oley refers to himself as a Cow Molester. I think that is an accurate description of what cowboys do. The definition of molest: to annoy and disturb.

When a cowboy says, "I'm gonna go check the cows," he really means is he's going to ride into the bunch, git'em up, turn'em around and just generally annoy and disturb them.

AFTERTHOUGHT: *Cow to bull: "I know you love me, but will you respect me next estrus?"*

ON GENERATIONAL DIFFERENCES

My daughter and her husband graduated ag college and took jobs in Kansas. After a year she called saying they were going back to college to get a Master's Degree.

I was shocked because of my own poor performance as a student, and I was stunned anyone would want to go back!

I told them I could get a job for them running a ranch right now, anywhere they wanted, even right here! They were good horsemen and livestock people and ready to handle anything.

She said they didn't want to work seven days a week, they didn't want to work 24 hours a day . . .

I said, "What's wrong with you?"

AFTERTHOUGHT: *I was visiting with my daughter on the phone. She was a sophomore animal science student at Oklahoma State. After pleasantries she said, "Dad, I think I've found the right man."*

I said, "What's he like?" She said, "Dad . . . he can weld!" My heart sang out! She's going to marry someone useful!

ON IT'S WHAT I DO

A cowman is the way he is
because he works with stock.
He's found it's best to ease along
to find the rhythm in their song
And not to fret if days are long
'cause cows don't punch a clock.

"A job ain't done until its done,"
that's life down on the farm
To gather those who tend to stray,
to treat the sick on Christmas Day
And if she needs your help, to stay
Until she's safe from harm.

You see you can't just quit a cow.
Sometimes you're all she's got.
No reinforcements in the hall,
no 9-1-1 to hear her call,
Just you, nobody else, that's all
To get her through the spot.

It's done without a second thought
by those who tend the flock.
"It's what I do," you'll hear them say,
with no demand for higher pay
And I believe they are that way
because they work with stock.

AFTERTHOUGHT: *And then there were the two cowboys
who threw paint on the protestors in front of the fur store.*

FOOD

FAMOUS WOLF RECIPE

ON COWBOY VEGETARIAN COOKBOOK

Fan Belt Fajitas: The most succulent fan belts can be found on old farm equipment moldering in your boneyard. It should be sliced into bite-sized chunks. Tenderize before cooking by soaking in fingernail polish remover. Fry in lard along with half a hatful of 3⁄4 inch black plastic hose and shredded playing cards. Serve with beer and jalapeños. It tastes a lot like abalone.

AFTERTHOUGHT: *John threw up in his plate . . . a perfect shot, filled it up. We all sat silently in a moment of expectation when the waiter walked up. "Are you finished, sir? May I take your plate?"*

ON DRAWING A LINE IN THE DIRT

Sam asked the judge at the Texas chili cook-off to dis-
qualify a contestant from Milwaukee whose recipe
called for noodles. "You've got to make a stand," he
said. "Goulash is good but it's not chili!".

AFTERTHOUGHT: *I like a woman who smells like BBQ sauce.*

ON FAMOUS CELEBRITY WOLF RECIPES

Woodchopper's Son: **Grilled on pages of Dr. Zhivago with oboe dressing, by Famous Wolf of Peter and the Wolf**

Fricasseed Grandma: **Presented on a red cape platter and basted with Geritol, by Famous Wolf of Little Red Riding Hood**

Typical Spoiled Wolf: **Meal of whining skinny juvenile served on a bun with sauerkraut, by Famous Wolf of the Boy Who cried Wolf.**

Blue Plate Special: **Bake one cavalry mule in a car fire for twelve hours, break the hide off in little pieces and serve with guacamole dip, by Famous Wolf of Dances with Wolves.**

AFTERTHOUGHT: *Ranchers welcome developers like hair growing in their ears or a skunk under the porch, unless, of course, they are ready to sell.*

ON VEGETARIANISM

How could you not like a vegetarian? It would be like not liking a monk, a Libertarian party candidate or a dairyman raising Jersey cows.

You gotta hand it to 'em. They are swimmin' upstream livin' life the hard way. But I admire those of them who are true believers. Even though they may secretly buy a Holstein, eat a burger or vote for Ralph Nader.

And organic farming? It's just some hard workin' folks that have found a niche. They have given up trying to save the world, they just hope there will be enough people in their congregation to keep 'em in business. Kinda like Episcopalians.

AFTERTHOUGHT:
I like chicken. I only wish it tasted more like chicken.

ON COMPASSION IN MENU LABELING

Rack of Lamb with Mint jelly $24.95 "Selected from an all volunteer flock in the pristine foothills of Colorado."

Salmon Gwendine $16.95 "Each salmon was helped up the fish ladder by wildlife candystripers in the Klamath River Wilderness."

Grain-fed Mississippi Catfish $10.95 "Catfish are fed individually and taken out of the pond to pee pee twice a day."

18 oz Texas T-Bone $28.95 "Each steer has his own personal trainer and is given poise and modesty lessons to mute his tendency to exaggerate."

AFTERTHOUGHT: *Which is worse?*

A. Being handcuffed and forced to watch someone butcher hogs on your living room carpet, or . . .

B. Being bitten by your own dog.

ON BEANS A'LA BLACK A TRIBUTE

"Speak to me of the humble bean
Of Milagro, of Jack and the Stalk.
Whose brave contribution has earned them a place
In the footnote of history's crock."

Quotes:
Recognized by poets, painters, bards and the literary glitterati like Shakespeare who said, "A bean by any other name would still . . ."

If a bean were consumed in the forest and no one heard it, would it still make a sound?

"One small bean for man, one giant bean burrito for mankind." - Armstrong

Gold, frankincense and pinto beans.

"I never met a bean I didn't like." - Lyndon Beans Johnson

"A fool and his bean are soon parted." - Anonymous

"Quoth the raven, 'Refried Beans.'" - Poe

"Hell hath no fury like a bean turned bad." - Congreve

"Bean me up, Scotty," - Startrek

AFTERTHOUGHT:
"The beef check-off has gone up to a dollar."

Misinterpretation: Not a bad price for a Russian sandwich. I know the Veal Solginetzen and the Chicken Zhivago are twice that much.

ON JESUS WAS A VEGETARIAN

The animal rights loonies put up a billboard pro-claiming, JESUS WAS A VEGETARIAN. I thought it would be followed by other 'endorsement' fairy tales like Moses doing a spot for bus travel. "Hi, I'm Moses. Next time you want to cross the wilderness in less than 40 years, call Greyhound!"

Or David doing a spot for the NRA, "If there had been slingshot laws in force back in my time, the Philistines would be in charge of airport security today!"

Others we could expect; Robin Hood proclaiming he was a Democrat, Buddha doing spots for Weight Watchers, Cleopatra promoting Coppertone sunscreen, Delilah joining Club Med, or a Virgin Mary satire. What's to stop some feminist group from using her image on a T-Shirt saying, "A women needs a man like a fish needs a bicycle."

And the ultimate billboard . . . God Smokes.

AFTERTHOUGHT: *Wine doesn't give me a headache. Winos do.*

ON TOXIC COFFEE

At the convenience store I poured a 20 oz styrofoam cup half full of coffee. Then I put it under the cappuccino chemical flavor dispenser and dribbled in French magnesium vanilla, hot cobalt chocolate and hazel-nut ammonium hydroxide. Then I took two each of the pasteurized, artificially-flavored, synthetic Irish crème, amaretto chloride and mentholated mint in their peel, spill and drip sealed thimble cups, and tried to splash their contents into the ever filling 20 oz cup.

All the while I was preparing my cauldron concoction, my taste buds were leaping in bud frenzy, doing gum-drop cartwheels and encouraging my salivary glands to wet their palettes!

Toxic coffee. An exquisite potion.

Right now I'm sipping coffee made from fresh ground Costa Rican beans in a China cup with real cream . . . and I'm wishing it had a big squirt of pecan caramel caustic cappuccino with a pH of 2. Probably not a good idea though, might take the enamel right off the cup!

AFTERTHOUGHT: *"To determine if an outside pool of water is good to drink . . . if it has bugs in it, drink it!"*
- Fred Edris

ON BABE

The movie Babe had a deleterious effect on the price of the *Other White Meat*. The sheep people know that it's hard to convince the public to eat something cute. Rabbit raisers are careful to avoid advertising including Bunny Burger or BBQ'd Bunny Ribs and Bunny on a grill. Even in the frozen north they've never developed a market for Baby Seal Club Sandwich.

AFTERTHOUGHT: *Sure yer waffle was tough. You ate the pot holder.*

ON NATURE FILMS

I've always assumed they were staged. I figured the crew gathers after breakfast and drives to a carefully selected spot. They arrive when the lighting is just right.

From the back of a used stock truck (with Nairobi plates) they unload an old antelope, a gnu with footrot and six crippled rabbits. The director signals to the truck driver and the prey limps out.

Then the director points to the animal trainer. He releases the leopard. Cameras roll...the leopard bounds toward the hobbling gnu, leaps for his throat and throws him to the ground.

"Cut," cries the director.

The leopard helps the gnu up, dusts him off and they go back to the truck. Everybody packs up and gets back to the hotel by cocktail time.

Isn't that how they filmed Jurassic Park?

AFTERTHOUGHT: *They say animal behavior can warn you when an earthquake is coming. Like the night before that last earthquake hit, our family dog took the car keys and drove to Arizona.*

ON WHY DO WE HUNT?

As Chief Real Bird would say, it is a deep primitive calling from a time, when time was not a word. It is built in our genes. Human beings are predators.

People who live in crowded cities can lose this instinct and take on the role of prey. Their protection is the same as a school of fish. The odds are that somebody else will be caught before you!

People who live in the rural country refine and pass on their hunting instinct. They are predators. When they hear a noise outside, they don't call 911, they load the shotgun and go out to defend themselves.

Hunting season is a part of this mentality. In the fall when we take to the woods and mountains, we are following the genes of our ancestors. If you ever doubt that hunting is not a sacred part of our natural being, go back and look at the drawings on cave walls. There are no pictures of people behind desks.

AFTERTHOUGHT: *How do you know the tracks were from a Spanish speaking person?*

The "h" in heel was silent.

ON GOOSE SEASON

Keith was doing fifty miles an hour when he flew through the flurry of geese. The sky was black with them. The raucous honking was deafening. Mud was banging in the wheel wells but he heard nary a shot from the hunters in the pickup bed.

In the blink of an eye he was clear of the geese, although it was impossible to see out the windshield. Apparently, in an effort to lighten their load, they had performed a cloacal evacuation as they sailed over the cab.

A glance at the intrepid hunters soon led him to realize why their guns were silent. They looked like they had been in an oatmeal storm. Maybe a Cream of Wheat drive-by creaming, or had stepped on a butterscotch mine.

Goose droppings splattered their Eddie Bauers, smeared their Land's Ends, coated their Cabelas, lambasted their L.L. Beans, splattered, smeared, blinded, bluffed and buffeted them as the blizzard of geese had flown over at ground zero.

Their spokesman removed his Smith & Wesson sunglasses, revealing the only bare skin on his face. He looked like a pallid raccoon.

"They shot first," he said, "We didn't have a chance!

AFTERTHOUGHT: *I asked why he had deer heads on his wall. He said, "Because I think they're attractive." I said, "I think my daughter's attractive too, but I have photographs of her." - Pat Richardson*

102

ON TROUTING

Not quite twilight. The tip of my rod silhouettes against a bright patch of water, it dips in rhythm with the current . . . or is it with the beat of my heart?

I feel the thump of a nibble. Or is it the weight banging on the smooth stones? Impatient I reel in. Part of the bait is gone.

Back in the water . . . in the sweet spot. The worm looks good enough to eat. I am convinced that I know what tastes good to a fish. I wait. He must be sniffing this tempting truffle, dancing in front of his face, the aroma surrounding him, flowing over his slick scales, filling his nostrils, his gills, I sense the moment, the impending strike, the expectation holds me still to the point of breathlessness.

The tip of my rod dips in rhythm with the current . . . or is it with the beat of my heart? It doesn't matter, they are the same.

AFTERTHOUGHT: *On medicating the water at a catfish farm, the receptionist asked, "How will they get the fish to drink it?"*

ON DO FISH FEEL PAIN?

The issue is not "do fish feel pain," but rather are they preordained to be eaten. Animal cruelty is in the eye of the beholder.

PETA, the animal rights group, contends that angling is cruel and barbaric, especially 'catch and release.'

Trout Unlimited defends fly fishing by citing studies that show, " . . . a behavioral response to noxious stimuli is separate from psychological experience of pain."

My advice to T.U. lawyers says that using scientific evidence in a debate with PETA is like trying to potty train a duck. Rule to live by: Don't treat lunatics like reasonable people.

Neither side can defend the simple truths. As any 3 year old can tell you:

#1 Of course it hurts!
#2 Fish have been part of the food chain since they learned to swim.

T.U. and PETA have the right to disagree, and it's not necessarily a matter of logic.

For instance, I think reality TV is cruel and inexusable. But, according to my logic, I guess some people are born to be humiliated, just like some fish are born to be eaten.

AFTERTHOUGHT: *Question - What is the difference between a flock of Canadian geese and a band of sheep?*

Answer - The geese know where they are going!

ON THE BIG ONE
THAT GOT AWAY BLUES

Since time beyond time they have sat 'round the fire

In the evening reliving the chase.
Offering prayers to the heavens above
For the swiftness, the big heart and grace.

Though novice or blooded, each hopes to himself
That luck will ride with him at dawn
'Cause a second...or step...in time...or in space
Is the difference between 'git' or 'gone.'

These primitive thoughts have clouded their minds
Since man started stalking the Earth.
The lore is passed down and is part of their soul
They have heard these same songs since their birth.

It hums through their veins. But everyone dreams.
It's what brings them here under the stars,
That primeval force they could never explain
As deep as the craters on Mars.

As the campfire light dances
and the flame still enhances
These warriors, tradition imbues.
By the glow of the embers
the teller remembers
The big one that got away blues.

AFTERTHOUGHT: *Slicker'n deer guts on a door step!*

ON CAN THE PUBLIC HANDLE THE TRUTH?

"Mommy, where do babies come from?"
"The stork brings them, Dear."

"Mommy, where does milk come from?"
"The grocery store, now be quiet and eat your hot dog"

AFTERTHOUGHT: *"They teach chickens to lay eggs by walkin' back n forth in front of them with a hatchet humming, Mmm, mmm, good, mmm, mmm, good . . ."*
- Doug

Out There

ON OUT THERE

I signed up to do commentary on National Public Radio headquartered in Washington (sorry, George) DC. The audience is very urban. I questioned the producer on why they chose me. He said, "Because you're the only one we know from Out There."

I always wondered if he meant geographically or philosophically?"

AFTERTHOUGHT: *I have spoken at the 75th Annual Southern Saskatchewan Sheep and Wool Growers / Combination Stock Dog Trials.*

ON AIN'T SEEN NOTHIN' YET

Mick owned a gas station on Interstate 80 in Hershey, Nebraska. One hot afternoon a sporty vehicle from Massachusetts pulled in and a fellow got out. He let his gaze travel the full circumference of the horizon around him.

"My gosh," he said to Mick, "This is the most desolate place I've ever been! There's nuthin' here!"

"Where you goin'?" asked Mick.

"San Francisco."

"On I-80?"

"Yep."

"Well," said Mick, "You ain't seen nuthin', yet!"

It is 638 mi from Hershey to Salt Lake City, the next city on I-80 with smog. Then 525 miles more from Salt Lake to Reno. There is a lot of nuthin' for the travelers to see.

The open spaces, breathin' room and big sky appeals to most who live out west. Like Mick says, "There's sumthin' about nuthin' I like."

AFTERTHOUGHT: *Suddenly, nothing happened!*

ON MOONRISE

I glanced up at the moon. The top third sat on the jagged mountainous edge of the earth's incisors. It was sneakin' up on the valley.

I stared a moment. Somethin' that big ought to be making a sound, I thought. Like a rumbling locomotive or creaking timber. Maybe the moaning of hi-line wires in a windstorm. I listened. Nothing but a nightbird and the distant humming of a truck on the highway.

I stepped up on the porch and looked back. The moon shone like a yellow headlight waist deep in a pool of dark water. Gonna be full tonight . . . then I went in the house.

I didn't have time to watch the moon hang itself in the sky. A scene so timeless it has been watched by Neanderthal men, Pharoahs, Moses, Michaelangelo, Columbus, even Pancho Villa and Garth Brooks.

But not me, I didn't have time. I had to make a call.

AFTERTHOUGHT: *"The sun with all the planets revolving around it and dependent on it, can still ripen a bunch of grapes as if it had nothing else in the universe to do!"* - *Galileo*

ON THE SIERRA CLUB

In communities where people ranch, timber and mine, the Sierra Club is about as welcome as anthrax or the pine bark beetle. Which is too bad. Because whether you work the land or admire the scenery from a distance, it is still a common bond.

I've always suspected that most of the urban membership, who do love the land, would be uncomfortable knowing they were not welcome in the homes of the people who live there.

AFTERTHOUGHT: *"Know how to make a big fire? Put out all the little fires for a hundred years!" - Sam Abernathy*

ON WYOMING MAIL ORDER BRIDE

She was a mail order bride, come to Wyoming to wed and love a self-sufficient rancher. Their mettle is strong as individuals but as a pair they are invincible. Louie and Ann have held together for 30 years through as tough a country and lifestyle as the West can throw at pioneers.

NASA is talking about establishing a base on the Moon. They are considering intensely the qualifications necessary for the astronauts selected to make this arduous journey.

My first thought was, call Louie and Ann! Give him a backhoe and fencing pliers, her a saddle mule and sourdough starter and come back in five years. You'd have a place good enough to build Wyoming a new community college.

AFTERTHOUGHT: *"Oklahoma Love"*

All she wanted a good night's sleep, a week at Tenkiller and a hot fudge sundae from Braum's.

He wanted to catch a bass, spend the night in the tent and marry this woman.

Farming,
Sheep,
Tractors

ON UNCLE LEONARD WISDOM

I was celebrating birthdays with Uncle Leonard. We shared the same one. When I was 44 he was 88. I knew his history well. He was born in Macon county Tennessee and at the age of 1 year old migrated with his family to Oklahoma.

One afternoon I was taking him into town. We were driving along a landscaped roadside bordering a subdivision. He pointed that way and said, "That's where me and my Dad started farming when we came out here from Tennessee."

I said, "Leonard, you were only 1 year old when you came out here. What did you do on the farm."

"Oh," he said, "I just milked and scattered manure."

AFTERTHOUGHT: *"If you've got good elimination, you got it made!" - Uncle Leonard*

ON MARCH MADNESS

March is the castor oil of months, the collected drippings of winter's oil change. The epic flush of the accumulated compaction of salted streets, sanded roads, gravelly snow and frozen manure.

In most of cow country it is a month to survive. A hold-your-own month. A can't-see-the-barn-from-the-house month. A soggy, windy, coughing, runny nose month.

It has its own ides; fungicide, blindside, cyanide, vilified, terrified, stupefied, snide, mud slide, hide, lied, cried, died, back you up against the wall and leave you flat and down, afoot and weak, and chapped and squinty eyed ides.

March is like playing tug of war with a team of oxen. They don't have to cheat to win. There is no way to beat March. So we just let it happen and occasionally we'll get lucky and it will let us win a hand. We should accept it graciously but never drop our guard. March is not to be trusted.

AFTERTHOUGHT: *Can you see a rainbow from both sides?*

ON FARM KIDS

FACT: The last census said that only 2% of the population of the U.S. is engaged in production agriculture.

Farm kids start learning the land and livestock when they are old enough to carry a bucket. When they help with the daily chores they are practicing.

Our culture expends a great deal of effort on NBA stars, astronauts, environmental lawyers and political science majors. But for every 100 rock stars, Rhodes scholars and Heisman trophy winners our country produces, we better make sure we spend enough to train at least two future farmers so the rest of them can eat.

AFTERTHOUGHT: *The list of essential professions is a short one. Most people don't get it.*

ON SECOND TIME AROUND

It's not givin' up, I told her,
just that we are gettin' older
And besides, the country's really
not the country any more.
We're surrounded by construction
that has zoned the mass destruction
Of our pastures and our neighbors
and our never-lockin' doors.

And we'll find a place less crowded,
where the air is still unclouded,
Where the country still is friendly
to our kind of pioneers.
Though the homeplace still might beckon,
they will ravage her, I reckon,
So we're better off just movin'
while we've got a few good years . . .
And are able to think clearly
and can still hold back the tears.

AFTERTHOUGHT: *"Burn your cities, save your farms, and your cities will grow back as if by magic. Burn your farms and grass will grow in the streets of every city in America." - Wm Jennings Bryan, 1897*

ON ALTERNATIVE USES FOR SHEEP

A replacement for a water bed; sleep on a Bed O' Sheep! Take them camping for use as a bedroll. They can reduce fire danger and you can count them at night.

How 'bout a safety device in automobiles to replace the air bag: in the event of a crash, a Bag O' Sheep explodes from the dash absorbing the impact then escapes out the door!

Other things come to mind like a large drain stopper, a self-propelled sponge or a place to store your extra Velcro. But the alternative use for sheep that may have the greatest potential: Q-tips for elephants!

AFTERTHOUGHT: *"Sheep are dumb. Which just goes to show you don't have to be smart to be useful."*
- *Pastor Blair*

ON THE GIFT

My daughter has the gift of remembering livestock. I can ride out in the pasture, look 'em over and come back in the house, and not remember what they look like! She can describe cows we sold five years ago! I admire people with that skill, or concentration or gift. I envy their ability. I wish I had part of it. I guess I have to be thankful that my dog remembers me and I can tell the family cat because it has three legs!

AFTERTHOUGHT: *The key to being fast is to be deliberate.*

ON RICH FARMING

There ain't no use me gettin' rich.
Knowin' me I'd spend it.
Then borrow more for land and stock,
there's plenty who would lend it.

I'm better off just gettin' by
and stayin' where I set,
'Cause the more that I make farmin'
the more I go in debt.

So, if wheat goes up to seven
I could sell it on the board,
but I won't, 'cause makin' money
is one thing I can't afford.

It's a different kinda logic
that allows a man to boast,
when the richest farmer farming
is the one that owes the most.

AFTERTHOUGHT:
"Farming isn't hard, if you don't mind work."

ON THE OTHER WHITE MEAT

Pork calls itself the other white meat. But it is interesting that on the graph of animal intelligence, a pig is to a chicken like a cowboy is to a sheep, like a border collie is to a turkey, or like a cow is to a rock. But what good has this intellect done for either of the species? They still spell ham and eggs.

AFTERTHOUGHT: *My grandfather had a friend who'd never raised hogs before, but who thought he'd give it a try. He was a meticulous man, so he read up on everything he could before he bought any piglets, and then kept precise records of every expense - transportation, feed, vet bills, sale commission . . . and in the end, when he sold them he found that he'd broken exactly even, to the penny.*

"Still," he said, "I had use of the hogs." - John Hill

ON TIME TO GO TO WORK

Have you ever heard a farmer say, "My gosh, I'm gonna be late for work!" Not hardly. They march to a different drummer. It's one of the great distinctions between urban and country. It is "Eight to Five" vs "Dawn to Dusk."

Cows are up at the crack of dawn, whenever that is. And farmers, like their animals, set their body clock on daylight and dark. The clock goes out the window. Ask anyone who farms and has a day job. Between waking at 6 am and doing chores, then leaving by 7:30 to go to work, anything can happen.

If there is any blessing in living life on nature's dawn to dusk schedule, it's that farmers never have to worry about overtime.

AFTERTHOUGHT: *Green grass has broke more ranchers than drought.*

ON ONE FARMER DOING
A TWO MAN JOB

Stretching barb wire to a post, holding it tight with your knee and driving in the staple

Hanging a 4 x 8 sheet of floppy paneling to a wall

Leveling a cross beam between two uprights eight feet off the ground

Pushing a cow down the alley into the squeeze chute then catching the head

Peeling your rope off a steer's foot in the middle of the pen

Buying every other round at the tavern

AFTERTHOUGHT: *He was so shallow, he had no depth perception.*

ON THE WISDOM OF COUNTRY KIDS

When my daughter was 11 years old we were raising rabbits. She was showing a new litter to her urban aunt. "They're so cute," said Aunt, cuddling one in her hands. "What will you do with them?"

"When they're about 5 lbs we butcher them and sell them to the grocery store."

Her aunt was aghast! "How can you do that!" she exclaimed.

My eleven year old looked up at her and said, "I don't make friends with them."

Wisdom as ancient as time from the mouth of a child. It is in short supply today.

AFTERTHOUGHT: *Smart as a busload of county agents!*

ON FFA LEGACY

I was at the FFA National Convention visiting with an ag teacher.

"How long have you been teaching?" "Thirty-eight years," he said.

There was a touch of weariness in his voice. We looked out over the sea of blue coats that surged through the huge convention hall. His wife took our picture.

"That's a long time to be married to an ag teacher," I told her, knowing the commitment a spouse must make to accommodate the late suppers, kids' projects, county fairs, field trips, night calls, weekend practices, long hours and exhaustion that are an accepted requisite of the job description.

She smiled and touched his elbow. "It was worth it," she said and walked away.

I looked out over the mass of blue jackets. They said there were 50,000 kids dressed nice, behaving responsibly, treating adults politely, not trashing hotels, yelling profanity nor abusing the hospitality of our Indianapolis hosts. The locals commented over and over about what a good group the FFA was.

That sea of blue coats is the legacy of the vo ag teachers and their spouses. They leave the world a better place. They have the right to be proud.

AFTERTHOUGHT: *"Mr. Advisor . . ." - Here by the Owl.*

ON HERDING INSTINCT

I sat across from a stranger in a restaurant who kept chasing his beans around his plate, crowding them up against the baked potato, keeping them together. I knew he must have some herder blood in his ancestry.

It's like raising a border collie in town. They are constantly in search of something to gather or drive or even just torment. Pigeons, cats, postmen, kids and even shadows fall prey to their primal instinct. Watching them you realize a big chunk of their happiness is never to be realized.

I had that same thought about the stranger herding his beans around his plate. He probably had an unsatisfied longing to be punchin' cows or herding swine.

Without thinking, I asked him, "Do you miss'em?"

"Yeah," he said, "Sometimes I just feel this terrible urge to go bite a hock."

AFTERTHOUGHT: *Two young, buff, studs said to the old-timer at the table, "So, what can you do, old man?"*

"I can pick up the check."

ON SIGNIFICANT DIFFERENCES
BETWEEN MAN AND ANIMALS

- You will never see an animal tip their waiter after a meal.

- It is uncommon to find an animal that has an interest in Western Art.

- Most humans avoid rolling in or pecking at pungent putrefying varmint remains.

- Animals don't smoke or chew tobacco after a good meal.

- Bovines cannot be taught to enunciate.

- Horses can whistle, they just don't want to.

- Chickens rarely have inflated egos, chapped lips or a future.

AFTERTHOUGHT: *Uncle Rass: "I don't see why I got to get my teeth pulled out and pay $30 for a set of dentures. I can get a perfectly good set for five dollars."*

Lyle: "Do tell."

Rass: "Yup. The undertaker over in Shell City's got two nail kegs full. Guaranteed fit, five dollars."

ON TRACTOR PULLS

The tractor pull contest is based on the deep philosophical question, "Who can drag a rock the farthest." Farmers have been dragging rocks since Cro-Magnon Bob cleared the first field in Arco, Idaho.

The cowboy equivalent to a tractor pull is the ranch rodeo. It is based on the concept "who can move a large, ill-tempered, hooved, horned beast . . . and not get killed!" Its prehistoric roots can be seen in primitive cave paintings. Remember the stick cowboy standing on the edge of the stick cliff waving a red cape as thousands of stick buffalo and stick mammoths mow them down.

The premiere event is the wild cow milking contest involving ropes, horns, hooves, speed, taking a punch, poor judgement and skull thickening. Substitute the word Woolly Mastodon, Cave Bear or Pteradactyl contest and you can easily picture the ancient mentality at work here.

Both groups still demonstrate skills essential to agriculture today which explains their popularity. The ranch rodeo displays roping, riding and branding arts, while the tractor pull continues to feature the archaic rituals of tinkering, buying tools and running to town for parts.

AFTERTHOUGHT: *The lazy don't get lucky . . . gettin' lucky ain't that easy.*

ON NOAH'S BOOK LIST
IN THE ARK LIBRARY

How To Get Ahead In The New World Even Though Fish Have A Head Start.

Practical Uses Of Animal Waste From Caulking To Finger Painting

How To Survive 40 Days And Nights With A Man Who Keeps Saying, "Pretty Good Ark, Eh, Mother?"

The Illustrated Guide To Sexing Amphibians, Newts And Domestic Fowl.

Noah's Captain Log Entitled, "One More Day Like This And I'll Never Get The Corn In!"

AFTERTHOUGHT: *"A backwards poet writes inverse."*
- Dan Flynn, punmeister

ON THE FARMER AND THE LOTTO

When Mel and Margaret won the lotto, the press took over, "After you found out you won," asked the bug-eyed press, "What did you do with the ticket? Put it in a safe? Take it to the bank? Bury it out back?"

"No," replied Margaret, "We just stuck it under the little smiley cow magnet on the fridge."

"What are you going to do with the winnings?" asked the reporter, breathless.

"Well," said Mel, "I guess we'll just keep on farming till it's all gone."

AFTERTHOUGHT: *A farmer named Simon said he wasn't in it for the money . . . and he had a lot of salesmen, bankers and relatives tryin' to help him prove it.*

Politics

And

Thanksgiving

ON POLITICS

Most politicians are lawyers. They specialize in obfuscation, clever sound bites, celebrity endorsements and a full head of hair. Maybe it's just me, but wouldn't you feel more secure if we had a president in the White House who could shoe a horse and weld?

AFTERTHOUGHT: *Political promises - They're like shaking hands with a pickpocket.*

ON ELIMINATING THE
DEPT. OF AG.

A political columnist said we should eliminate the USDA because only 2% of the population is involved in production agriculture. He says most of their departments could be eliminated and the relevant ones transferred to the Dept. of Interior.

If his theory is correct, maybe we should abolish the Dept. of Defense. Less than .5% are serving in the Armed Forces. Most of the machinery, tanks, guns, ships and planes could be maintained by Jiffy Lube and the troops turned over to the National Football League for defensive and offensive training.

The columnist would think my suggestion is preposterous! That the Dept. of Defense is essential to the security and survival of a nation. That any nation that cannot defend itself is doomed to third world existence.

Really? A wise man once said, "When you have enough to eat, you have a lot of problems. When you don't have enough to eat, you have one problem."

AFTERTHOUGHT: *Food aid to Afghanistan - Once again America charges into the breech of conflict with butter and breadsticks.*

ON STUBBORNNESS

We have been weaned on compromise, tolerance and turning the other cheek to get along with our playmates. The world teaches moderation, no rough edges, no eddies in the current, live and let live. A vanilla world without Tabasco, hot fudge, Bob Dylan or Jerry Falwell.

Then suddenly from the primordial pablum rises somebody who says, "I ain' buyin' into Beanie Babies, National Health Care and chasin' cows on a four-wheeler!"

Well, these purists often get mowed over, ground down or hoisted on their own righteous petard. But they certainly roil the water for a while and make us re-examine our own comfortable apathy for a time.

And sometimes in rare cases they alter the course of things for years to come, like FDR, Martin Luther King, Ronald Reagan or Bill Gates. They rolled into the stream like the Rock of Gibralter and changed the world.

AFTERTHOUGHT: *Remember, if you get into a fight with an old man, be careful . . . they cheat.*

ON ALTERNATIVE FUELS

The Department of Energy has taken on the daunting responsibility of eliminating dirty air. They are thinking toward a time when we do not rely on coal, gas, oil, solar, wind or nuclear sources. They are now doing research on biomass extraction. "Think of it," the Secretary said, ". . . lawn clippings, corn stalks, grass, oats and hay. . . and the emissions would be CO_2 and water!"

"My gosh," I said, "You're inventing the horse."

AFTERTHOUGHT: *If they were really concerned about gas guzzling SUVs and drilling for oil in the Arctic, shouldn't environmentally conscious politicians publicly applaud $10 a gallon gas as a means to stimulate fuel conservation? Oh, I forgot it's an election year!*

ON WARNING LABELS!

To keep busy, the government continues to search out things they can protect you from:

WARNING: Consuming more than 10 lbs of garlic a day for 25 yrs can cause a severe reduction in the number of party invitations you will receive.

WARNING: The Surgeon General has found that smoking unlit cigarettes may lead to meetings with boring people.

WARNING: The Sec. of Commerce has found that driving your car can result in secondary exposure to rude motorists on the highway.

WARNING: If you paid more than 15 cents a pound for this horse, you had better have a day job.

WARNING: The price of silver has no relation to the price of silver.

WARNING: The directions on this box are only good if you follow them.

WARNING: If you elect me you get what you pay for.

WARNING: Hanging out with dairymen may convince you that no alfalfa grower in the U.S. knows how to produce the kind of hay that they did ten years ago.

WARNING: If you go first when telling the amount of rain you had last night, it is written that your neighbor will always have had a tenth of an inch more.

ON MY LOCAL PAPER

I think of local papers as the last refuge of unfiltered America. A running documentary of the warts and triumphs of real people unfettered by the spin, the bias, and the opaque polish of today's homogenized journalism. It is the difference between 'homemade' and Pop Tarts.

It gives our little community a sense of place in the world. We are important to somebody. We make a difference. The paper recognizes that.

They are the glue, the mirror, the billboard, the flashlight, the semaphore, the boom box and microphone of small towns. It is how we hold hands. They care. They show us we care. They wear our heart on their sleeve.

Is it accurate to say that I really "love" my local paper? Well, it's not quite the proper word, but ... I can't think of a better one.

AFTERTHOUGHT: *Editors exorcise your writes.*

ON NATIONALIZING THE LEGAL PROFESSION

I have a brother with the ability to solve complex problems with the wisdom of Solomon. Something as simple as two brothers sharing what's left of the pie; one cuts, the other gets the first pick.

On gay marriage; allow them to adopt each other.

Now that we are nationalizing the medical profession, it follows to nationalize the legal profession.

Lawyers are the doctors worst enemy. If we nationalize doctors and the quality of health care declines for most, as the AMA proposes, normally there would be an increase in malpractice lawsuits.

But if lawyers themselves were forced to work for the same reduced salaries as the doctors are being forced to take, there would be a sharp decline in the study of lawyery (a branch of robb-yery.)

Cases would be decided by tribunals of appointed judges knowledgeable in medicine. We'd have to face reality; overweight people could not sue Ben and Jerry's, smokers could not sue Phillip Morris, and addiction of drugs could not be blamed on drug dealers.

Other occupations might be nationalized, like politics. People would be appointed to office; voting would be abolished . . .

Wait a minute . . . who would be in charge? Is Castro still alive?

AFTERTHOUGHT: *I decided to act as my own lawyer in my divorce proceeding and lost everything!*

ON MOTHER'S DAY

Behind those eyes there shines a light
That's guided me from my first step
Down life's highway through thick and thin
So I could tell what's wrong from right.

Behind those eyes there beats a heart
That taught me love is what you feel
And to be taken as it is
And not something you take apart.

Behind those eyes there lives a soul
That speaks to me from deep within
And warns me I must not despair
Those things in life I can't control.

Behind those eyes there is a love
That never lets me out of sight
And stretches from my deepest flaw
And reaches to the stars above.

Behind those eyes I see myself
The hopes and dreams she had for me
I see myself as I could be
Behind my mother's eyes.

AFTERTHOUGHT: *After outliving two good men, she said, "I knew what I had when I had it, and I knew what I lost when I lost it." - Theodora Ashby Black Tomson, 1919-2010*

ON THE FLAG

Ladies and gentlemen I give you the flag
That flew over Valley Forge
Was torn in two by the gray and blue
And bled through two World Wars.

I give you the flag that burned in the street
In protest, in anger and shame,
The very same flag that covers the men
Who died defending her name.

We now stand together, Americans all
Either by choice or by birth
To honor the flag that's flown on the moon
And changed the face of the Earth.

History will show this flag stood a friend
To the hungry, the homeless and lost
That a mixture of men as common as clay
Valued one thing beyond cost

And they've signed it in blood from Bunker Hill
To Saigon, Kuwait, Bosnia, Baghdad, Kabul and Toko Ri
I give you the flag that says to the world,
Each man has a right to be free.

AFTERTHOUGHT: *Salute*

140

ON RELIGIOUS REFLECTIONS

I was sittin' in a little country church. I noticed a banner on the wall that read MOUNT UP WITH WINOS.

Many thoughts raced through my mind but I figgered it was a New Age congregation. I began thinking up other phrases that might be acceptable: Ride with the Risque, Sail with Sinners, Lie Down with the Licentious, Commune with the Immoral, Huddle with the Homeless, Do Lunch with the Offender.

I asked my daughter what she thought of the banner,

"Mount up with Wings." she said, "Kinda cool, I guess. Why?"

"Oh," I said, silently vowing to start wearing glasses, "Just curious."

AFTERTHOUGHT: *If it's got wine in it . . . it's a wine glass.*

ON TAKE YOUR BELONGINGS AND GO

As fires, earthquakes, floods and tornados routinely drive us from our homes, it is a credit to our species that the first "belongings" most evacuees take, after their families are safe, is their pet. Not the entertainment center, table saw, sofa, swamp cooler, the silverware or the brand new cowboy hat. At the top of the list is Sparky or Miss Kitty. Mongrels with no pedigree, bad habits and a $500 vet bill.

In a world where so much emphasis is placed on material possessions, our relationship with our animals turns out to be one of our most redeeming features.

It makes us almost human.

AFTERTHOUGHT: *Disclaimer - No animals were harmed in the writing of this book.*

ON WEE THANKSGIVING

I was explaining Thanksgiving to my 3 year old son. We had worked our way through the Indians, the turkey and the pilgrims. "So now every year we have Thanksgiving with friends and eat a lot and say thanks for the blessings we have."

"Bessing? What looks like bessing?"

"A blessing? Sometimes it looks like a little boy."

"Like me?"

"Yup, sometimes it looks just like you."

AFTERTHOUGHT: *Hungry people don't protest genetically modified foods.*

ON COWBOY GRACE

You can believe I'm a thankful man
though it might be undeserved
And I'll eat whatever comes out of the pan
no matter what's being served.

So count me in if you're needin' grace said
and bless those who provide it
The farmers and ranchers, the bakers of bread,
the loving hands that fried it

But most of all, Lord, we give thanks to You
'cause we who work the land
Know how much our harvest and bounty is due
to the gainful touch of Your hand.

So bless this food and the life we embrace
and please forgive us our pride
When others with tables of plenty say grace
for what we've helped You provide.

AFTERTHOUGHT: *Amen*

Electamony

ON BE CAREFUL AND DON'T GET HURT

Be careful and don't get hurt. Joe Camacho is a cage fighter. Can you imagine his mother saying as he walks into the ring to battle the front line of the Oakland Raiders, "Be careful and don't get hurt."? All of us who work with large animals on the ranch or farm know getting hurt is inevitable. You get use to it and get over it.

And when Joe Camacho walks out of the cage looking like he has been beaten with a bagful of coconuts, is he hurting? What do you think? But he'd rather do that than sit in a toll booth on the turnpike for 8 hours a day . . . and I guess I would too.

AFTERTHOUGHT: *"It's not how much talk you do that makes you a cowboy, it's how much tack you've worn out." - Ed Ashursht*

ON ADMONITION

Never underestimate the common sense of the every-day working mother. She can spot a smooth talkin' lunatic quicker than the FBI, CNN or airport security!

AFTERTHOUGHT: *Thrifty as a single mother at a yard sale.*

ON IMMIGRATION

America stands for freedom. A word that never sounds trite to immigrants. They know its true meaning, the chance to be the best you can be. And to those who have always known freedom, immigrants remind us not to take it for granted. They know America does not guarantee happiness or success. It offers an even greater gift, the freedom to pursue it.

AFTERTHOUGHT: *"The dogs may bark, but the caravan moves on." - Rex Allen Jr*

ON POLITICALLY CORRECT COWBOYS AND INDIANS

There is a little town in Pennsylvania that is home to Juniata College. The college's moniker has been the Juniata Indians since its inception in 1876. Under politically correct pressure they changed their name and are now the Juniata Eagles.

The majority of the alumni are disgruntled about the decision, but they are acquiescing. One of them had suggested, what he thought was a good compromise, "How' bout just calling ourselves the 'Juniata Formerly Known As Indians.' It worked for Formerly Known As Prince."

AFTERTHOUGHT: *Why were the Indians here first? They had reservations.*

ON DUCK TAPE TESTIMONIAL

From D.W. poultry pathologist: Doing surgery on chickens is uncommon. Whenever I saw a chicken he was usually dead. And yet many suffered from ingrown feathers. Most polloqueros (chicken cowboys from Mexico) spend hours each day gently plucking the ingrown feathers from afflicted hens. One afternoon I was helping and happened to drop a chicken on a strip of Duct Tape I had circled around my feet to stave off fire ants. Inspired, the polloqueros completely wrapped me with Duct Tape, sticky side out, and slapped the chicken's afflicted area containing the ingrown feather against my body. This technique has since been adopted to de-claw cats, and in beauty shops as a depilatory.

AFTERTHOUGHT: *If we name hurricanes after women, thunderstorms after men and college football teams after snacks, what's next? Naming clouds after congressmen who make promises?*

ON RETIREMENT AT 55?

It's too young. They should be forced to suffer more anxiety, exhaustion and life-draining challenges; what's the matter with them? Retiring at 55 is like:

Decorating the Christmas tree to within 3 feet of the top.

Having one shoe shined.

Pulling your pants up halfway.

Quitting in the 7th inning.

Rotating just 2 tires.

Eating the artichoke and leaving the heart.

A facelift on just one side.

Clipping the toenails on just one foot.

Eating à la mode and leaving the pie.

Installing an elevator that doesn't go to the top.

Buying an engagement ring and not getting married.

Buying a cow but no cowboy hat.

Not finishing the marathon, the hot fudge sundae, the John Grisham book, the drive to Miles City, Marfa or Big Stone Gap, the letter to your mother, your daughter or the editor, especially to your mother.

AFTERTHOUGHT: *"So," I asked Dave, "How'd yer dad get that big dent on the door?" Truth is, it was quite an accomplishment for one single dent to stand out from all the other wear and tear, deterioration and assorted damage that covered his rattle trap Ford Ranger pickup like elephant tracks on a Styrofoam cooler.*

ON THE UNCERTAINTY PRINCIPLE

I have a friend who buys a new SUV every 3 years and I buy his used one! If one buys used cars you must expect to repair them. In one of my deals it turned out that it had a dysfunctional set of gauges. Either the gas gauge would work or the speedometer would work, but they would not work simultaneously. To fix it at the dealer required replacing the whole unit...only $400. I decided I could live with the problem.

Our son was 15, with his driver's permit. We were on a long country road when I suggested to my wife that we should let our son drive a little. She objected because my car wasn't safe, the gauges didn't work. I argued that was irrelevant. We discussed, as parents would do.

From the back seat came a 15 year old voice, "What you have is an example of the *uncertainty principle*." I asked, "What do you mean?"

"Well," he explained patiently, "The uncertainty principle says 'the more accurately you can measure the speed of a particle in space, the less accurately you can measure its location in space.'"

I responded, "Huh?"

"Yes," he said, "In your case you will either know when you will get there or *if* you will get there."

AFTERTHOUGHT: *"It's all physics to me . . ."*

ON EVERYBODY'S GOOD
AT SOMETHING

I have a set of golf clubs (including scuba gear, backhoe, chainsaw and eraser). I enjoy a good 9 holes, but it is hard for me to explain televised golf. It is like watching a haircut from 1200 ft!

"He's addressing the ball, Morton, a good 2 iron or 4 wood from the pin which lays beyond that dog leg to the right...he's got a bad lie there between the concrete bridge abutment and that 100 lb. Hefty bag full of Styrofoam ping pong balls...not able to get a full backswing he has grasped his club like an axe...the swing! My gosh, Morton, he's chipped the cinder block, burst the bag and the air is filled with a blizzard of white balls ... he's still flailing! Look out, Mor ... !" WHACK!

AFTERTHOUGHT: *Poor Jerry is a cobbler. He has a sign on the inside of his door. It says, "Thanks. Don't forget to drag your feet!"*

ON SYLLIJUNCTION

(def) a method of syllable conjunction to conserve words and paper, invented by Chris.

For instance, instead of asking "Does your innuendo about my behavior insinuate that you think I am guilty?" You could simply say, "Is that an insinnuendo?"

In syllijunction a combine becomes a *kine*, broke down is *brown*, and go to town for parts is *garts*, as in, "Honey, my kine's brown can you garts?"

Coy is Cowboy.   Churfer is Channel Surfer.   Capo is Couch Potato, Frep is Pharmaceutical Rep, Darmer is a Dairy Farmer. Simple enough?

"I'd like a cuppa coffream and two freggs with hown's and cakin'. (Hashbrowns and Canadian Bacon.)"

Log - Lazy Dog, Flot - Feedlot, Blangus - Black Angus, Perford, Jeer, Lane - Log Chain, Dow, Cormer, Triver, Brider, Neditor, on and on.

I'll leave you with this one.

"Insufferation injured at prest outside prodeo when barbrider boffs into her organigrown fruit and nut display. Both suffered blary and balnut stains. Thoodness noburt!"

AFTERTHOUGHT: *Black Cherry and Black Walnut . . .oh. Thanx.*

ON JAVELINA RAP

"These are javelina," said the zoo guide, "collared peccary."

"It looks like a pig," I said.

"Only to amateur wildlife wannabees," he smirked.

"Okay, Bambi Buns," I challenged, "describe a javelina to me without using the word pig, pork, oink, grunt, swine, University of Arkansas, boar or BLT!"

He couldn't. To the kids I said, "What does a javelina look like?" "A PIG!" they shouted in unison. I rest my case.

Today the learn-ed call something that rhymes, rhyming verse. They reserve the word POETRY for a "composition in verse, poetic diction, marked by elevation or beauty."

So, Longfellow, John Milton, Robert Burns, Poe, Robert Service, and Wallace McRae didn't write poetry, they wrote, "rhyming verse," unless it didn't rhyme, of course.

Which relegates me to a "cowboy rhyming versifier"

I believe the world is leaving the learn-ed behind along with the flat-Earth theory.

Ask any three year old what a poem is. They'll tell ya, "It rhymes, silly!"

AFTERTHOUGHT: *Pardon me, I was thinking without permission.*

ON BE THE KEY

For job seekers I heard a motivational speaker say, "Have the key to what they want!"

I thought, "It's not HAVE the key, it's BE the key!"

If I was consulting a wife because every Saturday night her husband drank too much, came home late and stayed home Sunday, I would advise her, "Don't HAVE the problem, BE the problem! Take a stand, show a little irresponsibility!"

Don't HAVE a headache, BE a headache! Look at the successful misfits who have achieved notoriety, not by bein' part of the solution, but by creating chaos . . . Yassir Arafat, Ozzie Osbourne, Geraldo Rivera, Osama Bin Laden, Madonna, The Riddler, Howard Stern, Ted Kennedy, Al Sharpton, Richard Nixon and Donald Trump.

Even death row convicts have fans.

AFTERTHOUGHT: *"When all else fails, "FALL DOWN AND BE SOMEBODY!" - Pinto Bennett*

ON POTTY MOUTH TRAINING

If one can get enteritis from eating with dirty hands, and lung cancer from breathing dirty air, can one get potty ear from listening to dirty words? And does one get potty mouth from cussing?

I am not on a crusade to improve civility between people. I can cuss in Spanish and English, and do when I hit my thumb with a hammer.

But I have no respect for the George Carlins, or Chris Rocks, or Ron Whites of the world. They do not make it a better place because they have no discretion, are coarse, clever, and vulgar. I regret there are so few movies or comedians I can take my family to see. The potty mouths have taken over the entertainment world. Books are no different; it is now commonplace for newspaper editors to show no restraint when quoting potty mouths, toilet tongues and salacious titillating purveyors of oral flatulence.

Our civilization charges on in search of the lowest common denominator.

AFTERTHOUGHT: *Funny as a dead mule in a car trunk.*

ON FINDING A PURPOSE

The kindest thing I ever do for my wife is to ask her to pick something up for me when she is going shopping. Nonessential tasks are so much easier if there is some purpose involved. It lets feel her good about doing something she is good at.

I enjoy bein' ahorseback. But I rarely accept invitations to just go riding. However I readily take time to gather cows, ride fence, go roping, brand at the neighbors or go hunting...as long as I can do it on a horse.

I've often wondered if martial arts practitioners get so tired of posturing, practicing and pulling their punches, that they slip out and deliver a few swift kicks or Judo chops to the occasional jaywalker or rude motorist?

AFTERTHOUGHT: *I'm taking up meditation . . . It's better than sitting around doing nothing.*

ON BAXTER BLACK

One of the most common questions asked of Baxter is, "...where do you come up with all that stuff?!"

He has spent a good part of his life entertaining some of the most independent, skeptical, hard-headed and gullible two leg-ged characters God put on Earth ... cowboys, farmers, ranch wives, sheep herders, wheat growers, large animal vets, barrel racers, horse traders and poets.

They are a colorful lot, usually have a lot to say, and have the tendency to step off into a wreck on a fairly regular basis. Baxter paints their lives in words on a canvas that never seems to end. Sometimes he gets spattered on his own self. Some think it gives him character.

ON WALLACE BADGETT

Wallace Badgett lives near Miles City, Montana. He's been a rancher, rodeo cowboy, deputy sheriff, brand inspector and college rodeo coach. Those who know him say he has failed miserably at all of it.

He likes to draw stuff, which has led to the creation of the syndicated cartoon, "Ranchin' With Earl." Wally's wife says this cartooning occupation seems to suit him because many years ago, when he was in grade school, he went out for recess and his mind never came back.

Recently he has decided to train his own Roman riding team . . . that oughta work real good.